First World War
and Army of Occupation
War Diary
France, Belgium and Germany

28 DIVISION
Divisional Troops
130 Brigade Royal Field Artillery
13 February 1915 - 2 December 1915

WO95/2271/5

The Naval & Military Press Ltd
www.nmarchive.com
Published in association with The National Archives

Published by

The Naval & Military Press Ltd

Unit 10 Ridgewood Industrial Park,

Uckfield, East Sussex,

TN22 5QE England

Tel: +44 (0) 1825 749494

www.naval-military-press.com

www.nmarchive.com

This diary has been reprinted in facsimile from the original. Any imperfections are inevitably reproduced and the quality may fall short of modern type and cartographic standards.

© **Crown Copyright**

Images reproduced by permission of The National Archives, London, England, 2015.

Contents

Document type	Place/Title	Date From	Date To
Heading	WO95/2271-5		
Heading	130th Brigade R.F.A. (HO V.). 1915 Feb.-Oct. 1915		
Miscellaneous	28th Division. Heavy Brigade Rfa A. (71th & 121st Batty R G A) Vol I 13-28.2.15		
War Diary	Woolwich	13/02/1915	13/02/1915
War Diary	Southampton	14/02/1915	14/02/1915
War Diary	Havre	14/02/1915	15/02/1915
War Diary	Poperinghe	16/02/1915	17/02/1915
War Diary	Billet On Vlamertinghe Ouderoom Road.	18/02/1915	24/02/1915
War Diary	Ypres	25/02/1915	28/02/1915
Heading	Heavy Arty. Bde R F A. 28th Division. Vol II 1-31.3.15.		
War Diary	Ypres	01/03/1915	31/03/1915
Heading	A/130 (late A/49th) Batty. R.F.A. (130th Bde R.F.A.) Vol I From 18 May To 3rd Sept. 15		
War Diary	Aldershot.	18/05/1915	19/05/1915
War Diary	Le Havre	20/05/1915	20/05/1915
War Diary	Sanvic	21/05/1915	22/05/1915
War Diary	Houlle	23/05/1915	26/05/1915
War Diary	Rubrouck	27/05/1915	27/05/1915
War Diary	Pradelles	28/05/1915	28/05/1915
War Diary	Strazeele	29/05/1915	31/05/1915
War Diary	Berthen	01/06/1915	02/06/1915
War Diary	N32a5.9.	03/06/1915	17/06/1915
War Diary	N.3.d.5.9	18/06/1915	14/07/1915
War Diary	Dickebusch Vierstraat N3d5.9.	15/07/1915	16/07/1915
War Diary	M24d10.5	17/07/1915	07/08/1915
War Diary	T2d3.3	08/08/1915	09/08/1915
War Diary	T3a.3.8.	09/08/1915	03/09/1915
Heading	B/130 Batty R.F.A. (Late B/89 Batty) Vol III Sept. 15		
War Diary	Landenhoek	01/09/1915	22/09/1915
War Diary	Borre	24/09/1915	24/09/1915
War Diary	Hinges	26/09/1915	29/09/1915
War Diary	Mont Bernenchon	28/09/1915	29/09/1915
Heading	B Batty 130th. Bde. R.H.A. Oct & Nov. Vol IV & V		
War Diary	Annequin	01/10/1915	19/10/1915
War Diary	Bas Rieux	21/10/1915	22/10/1915
War Diary	Marseilles	26/10/1915	27/10/1915
War Diary	H.M. Troop. Ship Knight Templar	05/11/1915	05/11/1915
War Diary	HMTS Knight Templar	11/11/1915	11/11/1915
War Diary	Mamura	12/11/1915	22/11/1915
War Diary	Alexandria	23/11/1915	02/12/1915
Miscellaneous	Appendix X		
Miscellaneous	M.O.I. Appendix XI		
Miscellaneous	Reference M.O.I Of 16.10.15 Batteries of 130th Brigade RFA will fire as follows:-	16/10/1915	16/10/1915
Miscellaneous	Operation Order No. 4. Appendix XII	22/10/1915	22/10/1915

WO95/2271/5

28TH DIVISION
DIVL ARTILLERY

130TH BRIGADE R.F.A.(HOV.)
1915 FEB - OCT 1915

121/4636

28th Division. Heavy Brigade R.A. (71st, 121st Bty, RAA)

Vol I. 15 — 28.2.15

Army Form C. 2118.

WAR DIARY
or
INTELLIGENCE SUMMARY.
(Erase heading not required.)

Instructions regarding War Diaries and Intelligence Summaries are contained in F. S. Regs., Part II. and the Staff Manual respectively. Title pages will be prepared in manuscript.

Hour, Date, Place	Summary of Events and Information	Remarks and references to Appendices
8.15 a.m. 13.2.15 Woolwich.	The Brigade left Woolwich by four trains starting at intervals of 1½ hours & arrived at Southampton from noon to 5.30 p.m. entraining the same evening on the liner Transport "Kelvin Grove". The weather proved too stormy to cross on the night of the 13–14 & the ship remained in	
2 p.m. 14.2.15 Southampton.	the dock until 2 p.m. on the 14.2.15 when she proceeded to her anchorage.	
3 a.m. 14.2.15 Havre.	At 5.15 p.m. the Transport got under way & proceeded to HAVRE; this port was reached after a good crossing, at 3 a.m. At 10 a.m. permission to enter Harbour was given. The dock selected for unloading this aeroplane was not suitably equipped for unloading many guns & vehicles & only one "train" could be used, the horses having to be led in & out to & out by another roadway. A floating crane had to be requisitioned to unload the guns, with the result that it was 12 m.n. 14–15. before unloading was completed.	
15.2.15 Havre	Orders having been received for the Brigade to move to Rail-head the 121 Battery entrained at 8 p.m.	
4 p.m. 16.2.15 Poperinghe	The train started for POPERINGHE where it arrived at 4 p.m. the following day.	

WAR DIARY
or
INTELLIGENCE SUMMARY.

(Erase heading not required.)

Army Form C. 2118.

Instructions regarding War Diaries and Intelligence Summaries are contained in F. S. Regs., Part II. and the Staff Manual respectively. Title pages will be prepared in manuscript.

Hour, Date, Place	Summary of Events and Information	Remarks and references to Appendices
4 p.m. 17.2.15 Poperinghe	There seemed to be a lack of cooperation between the Staff & Railway authorities, the time-table was worked with the result that the guns had no appliances to relieve themselves or to let them pass.	
1.40 am 18.2.15 Billet on Vlamertinghe - Elverdinghe Road	At 4 p.m. the following day the Battery arrived at POPERINGHE. Detraining was slow owing to the fact that the platform was constructed for the loading & off loading of the trucks and bombing, & the ends of many of the trucks were such "up down" with the result that severe shunting was necessary. It was 11.15 p.m. before it was able to move off to the billet - a farm on the VLAMERTINGHE - ELVERDEM road - where it arrived at 1.40 am 18.2.15. At 9.30 am 71 Battery left HAVRE arriving at POPERINGHE & going into billets on a farm close to that town for the night. During the 18th the Bde. Cr. reconnoitred positions for his batteries & selected his own Head Quarters. YPRES. 121 Battery tried to occupy the position reserved for it by 113 - the 71 arrived at the farm reserved for it near Hd Qrs of 3rd R.F.A. Brigade.	

Army Form C. 2118.

WAR DIARY
or
INTELLIGENCE SUMMARY.
(Erase heading not required.)

Instructions regarding War Diaries and Intelligence Summaries are contained in F.S. Regs., Part II and the Staff Manual respectively. Title pages will be prepared in manuscript.

Hour, Date, Place	Summary of Events and Information	Remarks and references to Appendices
19.2.15	121 Succeeded in assigning to position 71st Brigade Ruin, both batteries put into telephonic communication with the H.Q. Brigade at Chateau Zonnebeke — in the outskirts of YPRES — the Brigade was in communication with C.R.A. 28th Division	
20.2.15	71 Said to occupy their position after dark	
21.2.15	& put 3 guns in, as the 21st was foggy they were able to put the 4th gun in during the day.	
22.2.15	Both batteries in action, but neither fired.	
23.2.15	121 Battery registered on the enemy's trenches. Final information was an Hypres battery, use was being about 2000 × in front of the battery, being made of a Field Battery telephone for purposes of communication. 9 Rounds (H.E) in all were fired & two were observed to hit the trench. Range & bearing of the target were taken from the map, the former proved to be 3150 ×. 71 Battery made arrangements for opening fire tomorrow on various targets.	
24.2.15	71 Battery registered Ecoff Farm. Range & bearing were taken from the map; 6 (H.E.) rounds were fired, the line proved about 20 to the left & a range of 5400× was "just short." 08 rounds	

WAR DIARY
or
INTELLIGENCE SUMMARY.

(Erase heading not required.)

Army Form C. 2118.

Instructions regarding War Diaries and Intelligence Summaries are contained in F.S. Regs., Part II. and the Staff Manual respectively. Title pages will be prepared in manuscript.

Hour, Date, Place	Summary of Events and Information	Remarks and references to Appendices
10 a.m. 25.2.15 Ypres.	The 71 Battery registered the Chateau at O.4.a.4.2. 10 rounds of air forces were fired & were observed by the observation officer 3rd F.A. Bde. The Chateau was registered at 3°30' × 146½ East — 20° Elev + (A of S). Left men was sent to select a battery observation post.	
2 – 2.30 p.m. " "	121 Battery opened fire at German Trench — Range 3/50 × 16 rounds were fired — this working party belonging to this battery was hit while digging observation post.	
26.2.15	The Batteries exhorted to work in conjunction with an aeroplane, but none turned up.	
1 p.m.	The O.C. 71 Bty had a conference with H. Beorin R.F.A. re programme for following day.	
8.30 p.m.	Orders were sent to man the batteries by night.	
27.2.15	Orders received direct by 71 Bty to register down German machine guns in their main trench O.4.6. Bty, was ranged on the target by means of obm officer 3rd Bde R.F.A. — The intention being
10.30 p.m.	to open fire by night.	

Army Form C. 2118.

WAR DIARY
or
INTELLIGENCE SUMMARY.
(Erase heading not required.)

Instructions regarding War Diaries and Intelligence Summaries are contained in F. S. Regs, Part II. and the Staff Manual respectively. Title pages will be prepared in manuscript.

Hour, Date, Place	Summary of Events and Information	Remarks and references to Appendices
7.15 p.m. 27/2/15 Ypres.	A message was received from Head Quarters "telephones to batteries, to the effect that the Wick Infantry Bde were relieving trenches & that fire was not to be opened during this in fact unless by order of C.R.A.	
" 28/2/15	An aeroplane was to have observed fire for 71 battery today, but a telephone message was received stating that engine troubles had prevented the aviator going up in the morning. Late in the afternoon an aeroplane flew over the battery but no signals were given. 121 Battery did not open fire	

(73989) W4141—463. 400,000. 9/14. H.&J.Ltd. Forms/C. 2118/10.

121/4505

Heavy Arty: Bde RGA. 28th Division

Vol II 1 – 31.3.15

WAR DIARY
or
INTELLIGENCE SUMMARY.
(Erase heading not required.)

Army Form C. 2118.

Instructions regarding War Diaries and Intelligence Summaries are contained in F.S. Regs., Part II. and the Staff Manual respectively. Title pages will be prepared in manuscript.

Hour, Date, Place	Summary of Events and Information	Remarks and references to Appendices
1.3.15 4/nco	The C.R.A. sanctioned the use of T.P. maps with three pin left in as a temporary expedient. The New Grays frage on charge being ordered & equipment to Pepa lin; with. The T.1 Battery had endeavored Registering with aeroplane observation at 11.30 the B.C. proceeded to his observation station. The aeroplane not having arrived, the B.C. on an over-visited the Head Quarters of the	1
11.30.	Major Barne which were occupying the Infantry Btn. which were a-occupying the Trenches & arranged to lay a telephone wire from the Battalion H.Q. to the O.P. post. This wire was laid by 8 hours at 9.7.pm	
12.30 p.m.		
4 p.m.	121 Battery opened true fire for a German battery located in T.36.c.6.7. which was shelling the position of a field battery which was observation or the light hour also station in position or the light hour. The enemy fire ceased.	7
10.30 a.m.	The B.C. proceeded to reconnoitre the high ground in I.24.d., T.30.b., T.29.c. & T.34.c with a view to obtaining a suitable observation	
11.30	The last mentioned was ultimately selected	

Army Form C. 2118.

WAR DIARY
or
INTELLIGENCE SUMMARY.
(Erase heading not required.)

Instructions regarding War Diaries and Intelligence
Summaries are contained in F.S. Regs., Part II.
and the Staff Manual respectively. Title pages
will be prepared in manuscript.

Hour, Date, Place	Summary of Events and Information	Remarks and references to Appendices
2.3.15 Ypres	The batteries had been warning to employ to carry out Registration. The weather however proved too bad all day & no firing took place — Both batteries remained during the night. Casualties 35 & 82 Gr Waggoner & attached A.S.C. admitted to hospital	71/F.A.
6 a.m. 3.3.15 "	11/3/15 Major Rome the order T/F.A. 184 last night received warn not to be East of E.H.H.F. F21 O.30 a.4.2. at 10.30 PM opened fire on German trench in O30 55 immediately opposite our No 2 trench, but no damage was found in a satisfactory sense carried out although by P. Fuse was only walking any will being killed, a large percentage of rounces — The O.C. Royal Fusiliers told Mr B.C. that this fire had made the Germans different to them in the trenches — ..... in all were fired	

Army Form C. 2118.

WAR DIARY
or
INTELLIGENCE SUMMARY.
(*Erase heading not required.*)

Instructions regarding War Diaries and Intelligence Summaries are contained in F. S. Regs., Part II. and the Staff Manual respectively. Title pages will be prepared in manuscript.

Hour, Date, Place	Summary of Events and Information	Remarks and references to Appendices
3.3.15 1/pm. 1.30 & 2.30 3 pm.	121 Battery. This battery was shelled at 1 pm & 2.30 pm at 3 pm the Battery opened fire on the enemy trench in I 29 d 6.5 & found the range.	
4.3.15 " 1 pm	7 Hy. Battery. Communication between the battery & O.P. was broken during the night & it was after noon before this was restored. At 1 pm fire was opened on the German trench in front of No 2 & 3 trench, the range was found & the effect appeared very satisfactory. The observation officer saw pieces of timber being blown into the air & informed Major Barn that he was very hopeful for his fire & that it was the O.C. Cheshire Regiment told the B.C. that their fire here stopped sniping. The Infantry got later in the evening, what he had wished	

WAR DIARY
or
INTELLIGENCE SUMMARY.
(Erase heading not required.)

Army Form C. —

Instructions regarding War Diaries and Intelligence Summaries are contained in F.S. Regs., Part II. and the Staff Manual respectively. Title pages will be prepared in manuscript.

Hour, Date, Place	Summary of Events and Information	Remarks and references to Appendices
3 p.m. 4.3.15 Ypres	At 3 p.m. the B. Battery continued to register E.TK.H.O.F. Farm, but after 13 rounds was unable to spot that he had had a direct hit. Observation was difficult for same being a wire freely partially visible & gun had a blow back & was out of action for examination.	
7.20 a.m.	121 B'ty. The Battery opened fire on Trenches A.1 and 6.5 fired 117 rounds. P.S. ceased firing at dawn.	
7.45	At noon fire recovery shelled the Battery 24 rounds in all being fired.	
12.15 p.m.	Opened fire on HOLLEBEKE crossroads C.11.5.10.6. 12 rounds fizzite were fired Telephone wire was laid down to I.4.c.3.2. Lieut Breade to Hospital. (casualties 23951 Dr Breade to Hospital)	71 H.B.

Army Form C. 2118.

WAR DIARY
or
INTELLIGENCE SUMMARY.
(Erase heading not required.)

Instructions regarding War Diaries and Intelligence Summaries are contained in F.S. Regs., Part II and the Staff Manual respectively. Title pages will be prepared in manuscript.

Hour, Date, Place	Summary of Events and Information	Remarks and references to Appendices
7.30am 5/3/15 Ypres	71 H.B. opened fire at 7.30 am on the redoubt in front of trenches 26 & 27. This was registered & served direct hits recorded.	
10.30 am	At 10.30 am the Chateau was registered by O.P. for the 121st Battery — about well. 71 Battery telephoned to Bde. H.Q. & have ditted from there to the Battery, registration was completed, one round being observed to go through the window, the remainder very close.	
3.6 pm	At 3.6 pm 121 Bty opened fire on O 26 & 8 (by map). 7 rounds were fired. at 3.30 fire was turned on to O 17.0.7.6. 6 rounds fired.	
3-30		
8am. 6.3.15 "	At 8 am the 71st Battery opened fire on redoubt in front of 26 & 27 trenches, fire seemed most effective & part of the redoubt was observed on fire	

WAR DIARY
or
INTELLIGENCE SUMMARY.
(Erase heading not required.)

Army Form C. 2118.

Hour, Date, Place	Summary of Events and Information	Remarks and references to Appendices
10.30· 8/3/15 Ypres.	At 10.30 a.m. the Battery received orders to be in action against hostile Batteries in O.15.c.5.2 – O.14.c.2.9 by 12 noon. day. also to have 50 yards × 150 Shrapnel fuzes in the Battery. At 11.15 the battery was ordered to open fire on the above target. No 1 & 2 Guns were placed in positions owing to the state of their platforms. The heavy rain & wear.	
11.15 a~	The position after the heavy rain & wear repaired after of a shew. at 11.45 one gun opened out of action was turned on to target. The fuze elevation was turned on to target. The left section was again O.14.c.5.9. 0.15.a.5.2 & 121 Battery was ay.ed O.14 on B. 0.15.a.5.2 & 121 Battery cease fire was received at 1 p.m. cease fire in front of 23 division was	
3/p~	at 3 p.m. the firebar of 71 Battery adjusted with shrapnel buf 71 Battery adjusted with shrapnel buf 145 for corrector for was found to be 145 for. Corrector fuze elevation 100 × two pieces C.P. T.P. fuze. elevation 100 × two pieces Tzpellente	

No 2/6344 Gunr F. Ho 18342 G Bridge 17 No 36015 Ryan W Casualties
No 2/6344 Gunr F. Ho 18342 G Bridge 17 joined 121 Bty. Killed
No 40414 G Hodge E. joined 121 Bty.

No 14052 Gr O B Allen admitted to hosp. sick wounded

Army Form C. 2118.

WAR DIARY
or
INTELLIGENCE SUMMARY.
(Erase heading not required.)

Instructions regarding War Diaries and Intelligence Summaries are contained in F.S. Regs., Part II and the Staff Manual respectively. Title pages will be prepared in manuscript.

Hour, Date, Place	Summary of Events and Information	Remarks and references to Appendices
12.55 P.M. 7/3/15. YPRES	121 (HB) opened fire on Redoubt ※ Fired 30 hydrolite	※ Redoubt in O.3.d.9.6.
1.35 P.M		
to		
3.00 P.M " "	71 (HB) Fired 37 hydrolite on Redoubt. Large quantities of timber & debris were thrown up. Fire appeared accurate & effective. The battery stood by for aeroplane registration. None carried out. Shirty. Casualties. 71 (HB) No 19657 Gr J. Chambers joined.	
9.40 AM 8/3/15 to 11.15 AM	121 (HB) Fired 20 hydrolite & 1 shrapnel at trenches in O.4.a	
1.46 P.M.to 3.42hm " "	121 (HB) fired 20 hydrolite & 4 Shrapnel at the Chateau & trenches W of I.D.4.t.1.5.	
4.50 P.M. " "	71 (HB) fired 12 hydrolite in German Main trenches, result not nonparticular. Saddler Gr Hackney joined. ※	
	Casualties No	
7.6 AM. 9/3/15	121 (HB) Fired 20 hydrolite & 3 Shrapnel on Redoubt. Ceased fire 8.46 a.m. dammay stone Iron blocks	
8.00 A.M. " "	71 (HB) Fired 21 hydrolite on Redoubt ※ T direct hits were reported from infantry trenches. A lot of timber was thrown up.	
1.40 P.M.	121 (HB) Fired 20 hydrolite & O.I.T.S. at Redoubt ※	

Army Form C. 2118.

WAR DIARY
or
INTELLIGENCE SUMMARY.

(Erase heading not required.)

Instructions regarding War Diaries and Intelligence Summaries are contained in F. S. Regs., Part II and the Staff Manual respectively. Title pages will be prepared in manuscript.

Hour, Date, Place	Summary of Events and Information	Remarks and references to Appendices
2 P.M. 9/3/15 YPRES. 3 P.M. "	71 (HB) fired 15 rounds of lyddite which fell between our own & German trenches, at 3 P.M. fired a very effective series of 25 lyddite & 5 shrapnel on German trenches about 0.3 b.d., 0.4 a.c. Infantry reported 24 direct hits. Other officers reported large quantities of timber & some bodies thrown up. This was born out by Belgian officers observing elsewhere. Casualties Gr Meade (71) HB wounded. (from Hospital)	✗ Redoubt O.3. a. 9.5
7.30 A.M. 10/3/15	121 (HB) fired 20 lyddite and 30 shrapnel at trench in O.4.a.4.2	
7.30 A.M. "	71 (HB) fired 22 lyddite at Redoubt✗, 14 hits reported, beyond anything Belgian Officer in our trenches reported that direct hits were being made.	
10.10 A.M. "	71 (HB) fired 26 Shrapnel at above target, the guns were thought to be shooting consistently & the range was good but the fuzes (T.B.P. No 65) were most erratic. Only 5" effective T.S. were obtained.	
12.35 P.M. "	121 (HB) fired 30 lyddite & 30 Shrapnel at the German target finishing at 3.5. P.M.	
2.40 P.M. "	71 (HB) fired a few lyddite on a line about 1° more West of its former line. About 10 who were effective & a portion of the parapet destroying of	
3.00 P.M. "	CRA ordered & 30 Shrapnel were fired in search of the rear of the trenches. Communication between 71(HB) & the Obs. Officer was bad at this time.	

Army Form C. 2118.

WAR DIARY
or
INTELLIGENCE SUMMARY.
(Erase heading not required.)

Instructions regarding War Diaries and Intelligence Summaries are contained in F.S. Regs., Part II. and the Staff Manual respectively. Title pages will be prepared in manuscript.

Hour, Date, Place		Summary of Events and Information	Remarks and references to Appendices
All day	10.3.15 YPRES	Aeroplane registration. Neither guns favourable conditions. Cannoltis N° 21024 W/S² Beadle, 121 (HB) admitted to YPRES hospital, result of slight gun accident. N° 76708. Gnr A.F. Parker 121 (HB) discharged from Hospl.	
	11.3.15 "	Weather very murky till noon.	
12.30 PM	" "	121 (HB) fired 6 Lyddite & registered target O.3.d.4.6 (German Trench) Ceased fire 1.30 PM.	
2.50 PM	" "	121 (HB) fired 20 Lyddite & 20 Shrapnel at same target. Shooting appeared good & effective but difficult to observe.	
2.5 PM	" "	71 (HB) engaged the same target firing at intervals until 3.30 pm. Observation was difficult but the shooting appeared to be good and effective at least 6 trenches being made in the parapet. 2 enormous Lyddite were fired followed by 12 Shrapnel.	
Very murky until mid-day	12.3.15. YPRES	8.20 AM. 121 (HB) fired on trench O.4.d.5.2 until 9.15 AM.	

WAR DIARY
or
INTELLIGENCE SUMMARY.
(Erase heading not required.)

Army Form C. 2118.

Instructions regarding War Diaries and Intelligence Summaries are contained in F. S. Regs., Part II. and the Staff Manual respectively. Title pages will be prepared in manuscript.

Hour, Date, Place	Summary of Events and Information	Remarks and references to Appendices
12.40 P.M. 12/3/15. YPRES	121 (HB) fired 27 high explosive at the Redoubt ceasing fire at 1.55 PM having done extensive damage. — O.C. 121 (HB) reported "Apparently the Germans are not repairing the Redoubt" —	
6.55 A.M. " "	71 (HB) who had been lent to the 27th Division, to take part in operations, reported "Ready to fire" the objective being HOLLANDSCHESHUR FARM (N.18.L.4.8) and trenches in N.18.L. but the Observation Officer, who was at VIERSTRAAT, found the weather too misty to observe fire. One round of 8 by shells was fired at 10 A.M. but the O.O. reported that it was too misty for observation at 11 A.M. but the trenches were registered and afterwards the farm.	
10. A M " "		
11. A M " "		
3.5 P M " "	71 (HB) opened fire taking part in a general bombardment of the trenches by the Batteries of the 27th Division. Several rounds fell into the trenches and appeared to be very effective, the farm receiving 4 direct hits. Casualties. Major Owen commanding 121 (HB) was slightly wounded* whilst observing the fire of his battery	* On the head near the left eye, by shrapnel.

WAR DIARY
or
INTELLIGENCE SUMMARY.
(Erase heading not required.)

Army Form C. 2118.

Hour, Date, Place	Summary of Events and Information	Remarks and references to Appendices
13/3/15. YPRES	During the day 71(HB) engaged the same target as yesterday. No rounds fell into the German trenches. These trenches were very difficult to hit being practically parallel to the line of fire. The weather was very thick & observation was difficult. 32 rds fired.	
12.5 PM "	Between 12.5PM & 10.15PM 121(HB) fired 12 shrapnel at HOUTHEM. Casualties 121(HB) 2 leaves D Nurves O/C 54 & 119 were admitted to Hospital & HD WO 85 transferred to Base Staff.	
9.AM. 14/3/15 "	71(HB) fired 2DTS & 121(HB) 16TS & 4 shrapnel at wood in 1.35.d and at c/ wood D.5.t.	
12 noon " 3 PM "	12 noon 71(HB) fired 2OPS at wood in D.9.b and 121(HB) 2 OPS at wood in 0.10.a. At 3PM, 71(HB) fired 2 OPS at the wood round the Chateau 0.4a, while 121(HB) fired 2 OTS at the same target and then at the road from bridge 0.4a to edge of wood D.5t.	
5.30 PM "	At 5.30PM The Germans fired a mine and opened very heavy gun fire. The O.C. Cheshires asked for artillery support and 71(HB) fired 4 TS at the Redoubt. These were effective & the Adjutant of the Cheshires reported next morning that they had had a quiet night.	

WAR DIARY or INTELLIGENCE SUMMARY.

Army Form C. 2118.

(Erase heading not required.)

Hour, Date, Place	Summary of Events and Information	Remarks and references to Appendices
6.35 PM 14/3/15 YPRES	71(HB) opened fire on two artillery targets in O.14.c.9.9 & O.14.c.1.9.	
5.46 " " "	121(HB) opened fire RX on O.15a.2.2. & LX on D.15f.9.9. found 2 lyddite & 10 shrapnel, ceased firing 6.58 P.M.	
8.50 " " "	71(HB) opened fire on the ST ELOI Rd, O.8.d.8.0 & fired 48 T.S. and stopped firing at 10.25 P.M.	
9.4 " " "	121(HB) opened fire on road from O.4.c.2.3. to O.4.c.5.2. and fired 24 T.S. Stopped firing at 9.83 P.M.	
2.10 AM. 15/3/15	71(HB) fired 24 T.S. at former target.	
2.30 " " "	121(HB) fired 24 P.S. at pasird-B in O.3.c. May fired from at 3.15 AM	
2.55 " " "	71(HB) switched on to Scheinvonde O.3.d.4.9 & fired till 3.45 A.M.	
3.40 " " "	121(HB) opened fire with RX on farms B in O.3.c. & LX on farms in O.2.0.c.3.6 & fired 17 P.S. marching 50 & firing from 3.20 Stopped firing at 4.25 A.M.	
6.15 " " "	71(HB) opened fire on targets in O.14 9.9 & O.14.c.1.9 F stopped firing at 7.31 A.M.	
6.33 " " "	121(HB) opened fire on former target & fired 12 T.S. & 2 lyddite Stopped firing	

Signed A. Grover Capt

Army Form C. 2118.

WAR DIARY
or
INTELLIGENCE SUMMARY.
(Erase heading not required.)

Instructions regarding War Diaries and Intelligence Summaries are contained in F.S. Regs., Part II. and the Staff Manual respectively. Title pages will be prepared in manuscript.

Hour, Date, Place	Summary of Events and Information	Remarks and references to Appendices
6.00 A.M. 15.3.15. YPRES	121 (HB) fired 25 Shrapnel R.F. at O.15.a.3.6 & L.T. at O.15.b.6.6 subsuming concentration Shrapnel at 7.10 AM	
11.45 AM " "	121 (HB) fired 14 T.S. on road O.3.r. Shrapnel at 12.20 PM	
10.15 P.M " "	71 (HB) Switched to O.S1.b.6.8 fired till 1.16 P.M.	
12.45 " " "	121 (HB) fired 2 Shrapnel & 12 T.S. at enemy target Shrapnel at 1.10 pm	
1.55 " " "	71 (HB) fired on enemy target till 3.25 P.M.	
1.54 " " "	121 (HB) fired 10 P.S. & 4 Shrapnel on enemy target Shrapnel 3.54 pm	
6.14 " " "	121 (HB) fired 14 T.S. & 1 Regulation on enemy target Shrapnel 6.20 pm	
6.14 " " "	71 (HB) fired rapid fire on S.T.E.O.1. R.A. till 6.30 P.M.	
	Early in the evening the G.O.C. R.A. 25th Division himself called up the Brigade office & said that the Lichhoue had shewn by gas & smoke that the 85th Division had sent over to Thrush as 17 keep in touch the Germans &c. This was conveyed	
	to 15 Batteries	
	Casualties 121 (HB) 4trusher horses wounded by 2 seriously.	

Forms/C. 2118/10.

WAR DIARY
or
INTELLIGENCE SUMMARY.

(Erase heading not required.)

Army,

Instructions regarding War Diaries and Intelligence Summaries are contained in F.S. Regs., Part II. and the Staff Manual respectively. Title pages will be prepared in manuscript.

Hour, Date. Place	Summary of Events and Information	Remarks and references to Appendices
All day 16/3/15 YPRES	No rounds fired by either battery. A quiet day	
9.15 A.M. 17/3/15 "	The CRA ordered the batteries to load on the rounds running S 28 S E from St ELOI. No rounds fired all day. Aeroplane registration failed for both batteries owing to weather. Casualties 4 officers & 1 Rhodes, horse of 121 (HB) which were wounded on the 15th (attached to Hospital). One more horse of same bat. just received from Div Armn Col, destroyed by order of Vety Officer. No rounds fired. One horse lately arrived from Div Armn Col, admitted to Hospital.	
All day 18/3/15 "		
11 A.M. 19.3.15 YPRES	CRA ordered one section of 121 (HB) to be ready to fire on German high velocity gun in wood 1.35c. which annoys our trenches	

WAR DIARY or INTELLIGENCE SUMMARY.

(Erase heading not required.)

Army Form C. 2118.

Hour, Date, Place	Summary of Events and Information	Remarks and references to Appendices
2 P.M. 19.3.15. YPRES	Lieut General Plumer Cmdg V Corps accompanied by Brigadier General Browne RA visited the Bde Hqrs. O.C. 71 (HB) Reports Casualties last 24 hrs. 73635 Gnr Hurt admitted to Hospital sick. Gnr Meany through-out sent to Poperinghe in foal. Major Browne reported an Observation Post at I.31.D.1.5 from which fire from 121 (HB) on the mound at St Eloi could be observed, if required.	
7 P.M. "	CRA ordered 121 (HB) to be prepared to shell the German supports 1.35 a.4.1 to 1.35.a.9.8 while a field battery shells the trenches, on the morning 20th. Casualties 71 (HB) nil " 121 " 1 horse admitted to Hospital Column nil. Rounds fired nil	

WAR DIARY
or
INTELLIGENCE SUMMARY.

(Erase heading not required.)

Army Form C. 2118.

Instructions regarding War Diaries and Intelligence Summaries are contained in F.S. Regs., Part II. and the Staff Manual respectively. Title pages will be prepared in manuscript.

Hour, Date, Place	Summary of Events and Information	Remarks and references to Appendices
8.30AM. 2/3/15. YPRES	71(HB) opened fire awaiting Registration and during the day repeated the following targets with Shrapnel. O.9.a.0.0. Range 5800-5850. O.10.a.1.5. " 6000 O.14.c.2.8. " 6300	
10.A.M. " "	CRA ordered 121(HB) to open fire on 1.35a.4.1 to 1.35a.9.8 at 10.45AM.	
10.10AM " "	CRA ordered 121(HB) to open fire on 1.35c. (high velocity gun)	
10.18 " " "	At 10.18am they opened apparently with success as the gun was shifted to O.4b.4.6 after 1 Lyddite & 5 Shrapnel had been fired at it.	
11 AM " "	121(HB) fired 20.T.S. at the target ordered by CRA at 10AM. Obs Officer on 38 strand reported this series as "Effective". Series ceased at 12.15PM.	
12 Noon " "	Expenditure Report received for last 24 hrs. 71(HB) nets fired Lyddite 0 Shpl 18 121 " " " " " " 1 " 15 "Battery Shell forms"	

(73989) W4144—463. 400,000. 9/14. H.&J.Ltd. Forms/C. 2118/10.

WAR DIARY or INTELLIGENCE SUMMARY

Army Form C. 2118.

Hour, Date, Place	Summary of Events and Information	Remarks and references to Appendices
2.10PM. 20/3/15. YPRES	LXg 121(HB) fired 10 rds at HOUTHEM came at 2.40PM. 121(HB) was ordered to lay one Section on O.4.h.4.6. the high ground before mentioned.	
3.55 " "		
4.PM " "	O.C. 71(HB) reported that his battery was being shelled by a Heavy Battery apparently 5.9" guns. Magnetic Bearing 169°. and by lighter guns also. A pair was received in respect DOPP 2 6/92 S.B. set at 27 which appeared to be the correct setting. Following new emplacements reported by R.F.C. Guns firing O.20.d.9 J.31 d.3.4 New emplacements believed to be occupied O.20 d.7.8 Guns firing & count in report O.17.a.4.9 Agph Y.arks.new 0.9 d.6.4 New emplacements O.5.h.9.8 New emplacement O.6.a.5.7 Guns firing O.5.b.2.7 Casualties 71(HB) Nil 121 . 1 man to Hospital sick. 2 riding horses opened	
9.50PM.	Gunner No 5702 Dr W Lyttone (71HB) admitted to 11 Fd. S. Ambce	

WAR DIARY
INTELLIGENCE SUMMARY.

Army Form C. 2118.

(Erase heading not required.)

Instructions regarding War Diaries and Intelligence Summaries are contained in F. S. Regs., Part II. and the Staff Manual respectively. Title pages will be prepared in manuscript.

Hour, Date, Place	Summary of Events and Information	Remarks and references to Appendices
30/3/15 Ypres	121 (HB) Registered target J31.c.2.0 at 4400 3 rounds permit hit	1
9.45 A.M. 31/3/15	7 (HB) reported high shrapnel which to have been registered. This morning we stated (10 rounds) round were fired. When that there were German filessneaching over & have no IT observers [illegible] to the army [illegible] on yesterday but think so". N.B. 14 years [illegible] Jan C. during the morning. Brig Gen Willock G.O.C. 46th Div BnB artillery (Northern). Registration was interfered by the ironworks German aeroplanes which [illegible] over position the morning.	
	Registered target O.17.d.4.9. Battery 121 (HB) rounds 10 of these 4 were direct hits at 13.10 P.M.	
	8 in orders fire to be [illegible] on Houthem. 121 (HB) fired 10 rds firmed Common Lothian 12.25 & 12.35	
12.25 p.m.		
	O.C. 121 (HB) reports German Mourrair following up. 13° E. of HOUTHEM.	

WAR DIARY or INTELLIGENCE SUMMARY.

Army Form C. 2118.

(Erase heading not required.)

Hour, Date, Place	Summary of Events and Information	Remarks and references to Appendices
6.30 P.M. 21/3/15 YPRES	Brig Genl Nicholls visited Hy Bde Hqrs & went with Colonel Brown to 121 (HB).	
5 P.M. " "	Moreuil de Sale returned from Sick leave.	
6 P.M. " "	Aeroplane Registration Reports received as below.	
	71 (HB) Registered O.10.b.0.6 many 6250	
	" " O.15.b.8.5 " 6600	
	" " O.12.d.7.9 " 3200	
	121 " HOUTHEM X roads " 3208	
	R.F.C. report run at O.17.c.5.5. O.17.b.2.8. & O.17.c.7.8. Marks last probably howitzers about O.6a.5.8 & O.31.c.8.4 new emplacements O.23.b.5.6. Guns O.22.a.5.7 still in position.	
	Casualties 121 (HB) Gr Whittall admitted to Hospital sick. 19th Ammunition Column 1 man to Hospital sick 21 Inf.	
10 p.m. " "		
10.30 P.M. " "	CRA ordered a Section of each battery to be laid on the Roads immediately South of ST ELOI. O.C Bde ordered 1 Section 71(HB) onto the S.W Rd & the whole of 121(HB) onto the S.E Rd.	

WAR DIARY
or
INTELLIGENCE SUMMARY.

(Erase heading not required.)

Army Form C. 2118.

Instructions regarding War Diaries and Intelligence Summaries are contained in F.S. Regs., Part II. and the Staff Manual respectively. Title pages will be prepared in manuscript.

Hour, Date, Place	Summary of Events and Information	Remarks and references to Appendices
22.3.15 YPRES	Both batteries registering by aeroplane all day.	
	71 (HB) reports Corpyts registered.	
	O.17.4.9 ranges Mounted Common 8150	
	O.5.4.8 " Sharnhoul 6650	
	121 (HB) reports targets registered.	
	Cross Roads Hollebeke O.11.4.10.6 Ranges 5600 Corrector 160	
	Ypres O.5.4.2.7 " 4500 " 165	
	" J.31d.3.4 " 4200 " 165	
11.PM	C.R.A. ordered a section from each battery to be ready to fire on the roads S. of ST ELOI & to be ready to do so within further orders. O.C. Bde ordered one Section 71 (HB) into road SW & the whole of 121 (HB) onto the road SE of ST ELOI. Casualties nil.	

WAR DIARY
or
INTELLIGENCE SUMMARY.
(Erase heading not required.)

Army Form C. 2118.

Hour, Date, Place	Summary of Events and Information	Remarks and references to Appendices
4.30 AM. 23/3/15. YPRES	At 4.30am the O.C. Brigade visited the telephone room & found Sgt Major Surry, whose tour of duty it then was, lying down. He placed him under close arrest & ordered for Court Martial. Sgt Major Surry was sent to O.C. 121 (HB) for custody after dinner.	
10.10 AM " "	71 (HB) fired 6 pointed Common on 0.17 d 2.8	
10.55 " " "	71 (HB) " 6 " " " 0.9.d.0.4	
11.50 " " "	71 (HB) ordered to report as above with T.S.	
12.15 noon " "	71 (HB) one section on 0.9.d.0.4 & one section on 0.9 a 0 0 fired 6 TS at each, stopped firing 12.24.	
12.26 " " "	121 (HB) fired 12 Shrapnel on 0.16 a. 1.4, stopped 12.34. Registration with aeroplane, 71 (HB) registered O.9.d. 3.4 range 5800 Corrector 165. 6500 Shrapnel. O.9.d. 0.4 " 6150 6650 Lyddite. Hollebeke Chateau, 0.12 d.5. range 8150. 121 (HB) Reported. Registration NIL.	

WAR DIARY
or
INTELLIGENCE SUMMARY.
(Erase heading not required.)

Army Form C. 2118.

Hour, Date, Place	Summary of Events and Information	Remarks and references to Appendices
All day 24.3.15. YPRES	Weather too bad for Aeroplane Observation. Casualties. 71(HB) No 51573 Gr Brown (Ammn Col) sick to Hospital. On move in field to Poperinghe. 121(HB) Gnr Manny & Horse shot one H.D. to Hospital. Ammunition Columns two horses H.D. shot.	
5.55 am 25.3.15	71(HB) fired 10 T.S. at Outposts 3.4 and O.10.a.11.5 and 121(HB) at Outposts. O.11.c.6.5.	
9.30 "	71(HB) fired 10 TS at O.9.b.3.4.	
10.40 "	121(HB) fired on O.4.b.26.	
2.20 pm	Both batteries ordered to layer the Outpost O.14.d.11.5	
3.30 "	71(HB) repeated above fired 10 rds founded Gunners 5/which were nearly all dire.	
4.55 "	Ordered 71(HB) to fire 6 TS at O.10.a.11.5 & 6 TS at O.11.d.4.9 and 121(HB) to fire 12 TS at O.11.c.6.5 & 10 TS at O.11.c.2.4.	

Army Form C. 2118.

WAR DIARY
or
INTELLIGENCE SUMMARY.
(Erase heading not required.)

Instructions regarding War Diaries and Intelligence Summaries are contained in F.S. Regs., Part II. and the Staff Manual respectively. Title pages will be prepared in manuscript.

Hour, Date, Place	Summary of Events and Information	Remarks and references to Appendices
4.15 PM. 25/3/15. YPRES	Both batteries "Stood". 121 (HB) to fire 10 rounds at P.10.9.2.0	
	71 (HB) and adversary fired 5 rounds.	
5.5 PM. " "	121 (HB) fired 5 rounds at O.11.b.6.4.	
5.22 PM " "	Stop fluing. 121 (HB) emptied one section on O.17.d..2.8.	
	Aeroplane Reconnaissance Nil.	
	Casualties. 71 (HB) 121 (HB) Personnel gunner now evacuated to Hospital. NIL.	
10.28 AM. 26/3/15 "	71 (HB) opened fire 6 rounds T.S. on targets	
	No. 79 = O.10.a..1.5. 102 = O.10.b.0.6 & 108 = O.9.b.1.34 A field General C.M. assembled at Hypo Hy Entry	
10. AM. " "	Bde to trial of Bde S/Major Scarry	
12.5 PM " " 10.30 HM	121 (HB) ordered to open fire on target 84 = D.31.c.2.0	

WAR DIARY
or
INTELLIGENCE SUMMARY.
(Erase heading not required.)

Army Form C. 2118.

Instructions regarding War Diaries and Intelligence Summaries are contained in F.S. Regs., Part II. and the Staff Manual respectively. Title pages will be prepared in manuscript.

Hour, Date, Place	Summary of Events and Information	Remarks and references to Appendices
9.6.3.15.	At Zonnebeke. Registered Sm. 71 (HB) and Hy. 121 (HB)	
	O.17. C.7.8. – mean number	
	O.17.8.28 Ranges 6800	
	Casualties – rank to hospital one man from 71 HB from 121. one from Column.	
		6500
21/3/15.	Guns all registered. Hy. 121 (HB) at 9.15 A.M.	
	O.9.6.49 Range 6600, at 9.30 A.M. O.10b.06.	
	Range queried. Sm. 71 (HB) at 1.14 P.M. O.17.d.7.9 Range 7150	
	71 (HB) reported Aeroplane situated O.9.6.49 at 1.5 P.M.	
		6125
	Ranges 6495 + 0.9.6.15 at 1.26 P.M. if not identified	
	with registration of O.17.c.1.4	
	O.C. 121 (HB) reports that the White shed on the church at Zillebeke two or three days ago [illegible] to 3.40 and now to 3. It is being watched for further moves.	
2.2.9.15	O.10 a.25 a building in action was hit twice by 71 (HB)	

Army Form C. 2118.

WAR DIARY
or
INTELLIGENCE SUMMARY.
(Erase heading not required.)

Instructions regarding War Diaries and Intelligence Summaries are contained in F. S. Regs., Part II. and the Staff Manual respectively. Title pages will be prepared in manuscript.

Hour, Date, Place	Summary of Events and Information	Remarks and references to Appendices
7.30 PM. 27.3.15. YPRES	Ordered both batteries to be ready laid tomorrow morning on wood in 0.17 and when aeroplane gives Fire, 71 to fire 4 Common & 121, 4 T.S. in hope of doing damage. Casualties 121(HB) one man to hospital.	
6.13 am 28.3.15 " 8.18 " "	Both batteries fired as above ordered. Targets Registered. 121(HB) J 31 d 4.7 Range 4525 71(HB) O 10 d 4.3 " 7000 Casualties 71(HB) 1 man civilian gyd from Hospl 121(HB) Gr Hooke wounded by a German huge which he picked up & exploded, admitted to Hospital. 121(HB) 1 heavy draught-horse died 7HD horses & 1 rider gunned	

WAR DIARY
or
INTELLIGENCE SUMMARY.
(Erase heading not required.)

Army Form C. 2118.

Hour, Date, Place	Summary of Events and Information	Remarks and references to Appendices
8.30 A.M. 24/3/15 YPRES	121 (HB) relieved German Battery wh. 71 (HB) opened fire on Order of B/greed. 6 T.S. 121 (HB) ... 6 T.S. ...was apparently ranging on the forms of hostile aircraft and only finished the order at 11.20 A.M.	
10.6		
11.16		
3.40 p.m.	71(HB) was ordered to fire 4 rds T.S. from each station at targets O4c 9.5 and O9f 3.4. there were apparently fired at 6 pm. 121(HB) fired 4 T.S. from each station at O10 b 6.6 O17 d 4.8. they fired at 6.6 pm. Four targets been reported by 5 pm as registered. 71(HB) was then ordered to fire 4 rds T.S. at O10 d 2.7 which they did and fired at 6.31 P.M. Our last Registration 71(HB) O.5.b.4. aim ... 6700 and O.15 .... at 6700. Casualties 71(HB) 4. HB horses forward 121(HB) 1 man from Y... Lieut. Col. I.H.P... to Hq Hospital C.	

WAR DIARY
or
INTELLIGENCE SUMMARY.
(Erase heading not required.)

Army Form C. 2118.

Hour, Date, Place	Summary of Events and Information	Remarks and references to Appendces
11.30 A.M. 30.3.15. YPRES	121(HB) 91 stores to fire bursts TS at J.31.c.0.6. then opened fire at 11.50 but had to stop owing to presence of hostile aeroplane. Fire resumed 5 mins when ordered to stop by the Brigade Major at 12.40 P.M.	
12.13 P.M. "	71 (HB) ordered to fire bursts TS at O56.57 and O56.4.6. they had fired 4 bursts when ordered to stop at 12.40 P.M. by Brigade Major. Aeroplane Registration 71(HB) O16.c.7.1 range 8600 ⎫ " O22.a.8.7 " 8150 ⎬ common pts " O23.a.5.9 " 8300 ⎭ 121(HB) P1.a.2.0 " 5400 " O5a.10.0 " 4400 " J32.c.2.7 " 4600 Casualties 71(HB) 1 Cat destroyed 121(HB) Corpl Smith admitted to Hospital MK Column. M.L.	

WAR DIARY
or
INTELLIGENCE SUMMARY.
(Erase heading not required.)

Army Form C. 2118.

Instructions regarding War Diaries and Intelligence Summaries are contained in F.S. Regs., Part II. and the Staff Manual respectively. Title pages will be prepared in manuscript.

Hour, Date, Place	Summary of Events and Information	Remarks and references to Appendices
2.50 P.M. 31.3.15. YPRES	Ordered one Section 121(HB) to employ fire yet when of 71(HB) to fire 10 rds T.S. and one section of 71(HB) to fire 10 rds T.S. at — O.15.7 – 5.3.	
3.15 "	121(HB) reported the 10 rds T.S. fired.	
3.20 "	71(HB) " "	
4.45 "	Ordered 71(HB) to fire 5 rds T.S. at each of the four points: O.15.Y. 3. 4 O.15.Y. 5. 8 O.15.7. 5. O.15.7. 5.	
5.3 "	This was reported as finished at 5.3 P.M. Our planes Reported enemy's trenches (when shown by dots) at M1(HB)–O.9.d.gd.I.a.m. O.15.a.8.4 run y 7500. & 101(HB)–O.9.b.9.4 run y 6250. O10d.6 Trun y 6250 & O9.c.4.1 run y 6700. The aeroplane observer reported that "many batteries (not hostile) were firing with black smoke & 18 shrapnel	

(73989) W4141—463. 400,000. 9/14. H.&J.Ltd. Forms/C. 2118/10.

121/0801

28th KNOWN

14th Divn till June 17; then transferred

Also (late A/Adj to Batty. R.F.A. (130th Bde R.F.A)
to L
From 16 May to 3rd Sep/15

Army Form C. 2118

WAR DIARY
or
INTELLIGENCE SUMMARY.
(Erase heading not required.)

Instructions regarding War Diaries and Intelligence Summaries are contained in F. S. Regs., Part II. and the Staff Manual respectively. Title pages will be prepared in manuscript.

Place	Date	Hour	Summary of Events and Information	Remarks and references to Appendices
ALDERSHOT	Tues 18/5		The 49th Brigade R.F.A. received orders for departure overseas. General packing up.	
			The Batteries of the Brigade were leaving Aldershot throughout the night -	
			Order: - B, C, D, and A (Brigade Hqs also) respectively.	(3CCJ)
			The first train of R/49 left about 11 pm	
	Wed			
ALDERSHOT 19/5		6.55 am	A/49 of Brigade Hqs were the last to go. The trains left the government siding at 6.55 am and 7.55 am respectively - the right section departed by the first train and the left section by the second.	(3CCJ)
			The port of embarkation was SOUTHAMPTON	
			The Officers	
		approx 4 pm	The Battery (less Lieut P.S.C. Campbell-Johnston R.F.A. and 65 N.C.O.s & men) crossed on the "COURTFIELD".	
			Lieut. P.S.C. Campbell-Johnston R.F.A. and 65 N.C.O.s and men crossed on the "MONA QUEEN" (Isle of Man Steam Packet Co.)	(PSCCJ)

Army Form C. 2118

Instructions regarding War Diaries and Intelligence Summaries are contained in F. S. Regs., Part II. and the Staff Manual respectively. Title pages will be prepared in manuscript.

WAR DIARY
INTELLIGENCE SUMMARY.
(Erase heading not required.)

Place	Date	Hour	Summary of Events and Information	Remarks and references to Appendices
LE HAVRE	Thurs 20/5	Approx 3 pm.	Port of disembarkation was LE HAVRE. The Battery having disembarked, marched to SANVIC, (a rest camp) where the night was spent. (PSC-)	
SANVIC	Fri 21/5		About noon the Battery entrained at Pt 3 goods station - of LE HAVRE. The train left about 3 pm. - journey via ROUEN - ARBEVILLE - BOULOGNE. (PSC-)	
		3 pm		
		9 pm	One hours halt at MONTEROULIER - BUSHY	
	Sat 22/5	Approx 4 am	One hours halt at ABBEVILLE.	
		Approx 8 am	Detrained at ST OMER and marched to HOULLE, some six miles NE of ST OMER.	
HOULLE	Sun 23/5		Fine and warm. - excellent place for concentration.	

Army Form C. 2118

WAR DIARY
INTELLIGENCE SUMMARY.
(Erase heading not required.)

Instructions regarding War Diaries and Intelligence Summaries are contained in F. S. Regs., Part II. and the Staff Manual respectively. Title pages will be prepared in manuscript.

Place	Date	Hour	Summary of Events and Information	Remarks and references to Appendices
HOULLE	Mon 24/5		Excellent weather	PSC(?)
HOULLE	Tues 25/5		The battery was paid.	PSC(?)
HOULLE	Wed 26/5		Fine	PSC(?)
RUBROUCK	Thurs 27/5		The brigade had orders to move - proceeded to RUBROUCK via WATTEN - VOLKERINCKHOVE and billeted the night there	
PRADELLES	Fri 28/5	7.30 am	The brigade left RUBROUCK and proceeded to PRADELLES via CASSEL. A/49 staff happened to be billeted in the commune of STRAZEELE	
STRAZEELE	Sat 29/5		Fine	
STAZEELE	Sun 30/5		Major G.M. Bridges, 2/Lt P.R. Hughes and 20 NCO.s and men sent to the 129 Bt (How) battery near YPRES for a few days	PSC(?)

WAR DIARY
INTELLIGENCE SUMMARY.
(Erase heading not required.)

Army Form C. 2118

Instructions regarding War Diaries and Intelligence Summaries are contained in F. S. Regs., Part II. and the Staff Manual respectively. Title pages will be prepared in manuscript.

Place	Date	Hour	Summary of Events and Information	Remarks and references to Appendices
STRAZEELE	Sun 30/5 and Mon 31/5		instruction	Ref Map. B Series. Sheet 28. S W. 1:20,000. PSC.J
	Tues 1/6	9.30 am	The brigade (less officers, N.C.O.'s & men attached for instruction its batteries in action) left PRADELLES and proceeded to BERTHEN via METEREN. 2/Lieut. S.A.H. Jones with about 20 N.C.O.'s and men marched to DRANOUTRE: here they were joined by the detachment which had been to the 18th (How) Battery for instruction. The whole started preparing a position at T.2 & 8.6.	PSCC.J PSCC.J PSCC.J
BERTHEN	Wed 2/6	10.30 am	At 10.30 am the guns and wagons etc left BERTHEN and proceeded to "G" Battery R.H.A.'s wagon line at T.1.6. 2.4. near DRANOUTRE.	
		9.15 pm	At night the guns were brought into action at T.2 & 8.6 and	

WAR DIARY
INTELLIGENCE SUMMARY

(Erase heading not required.)

Army Form C. 2118

Instructions regarding War Diaries and Intelligence Summaries are contained in F.S. Regs., Part II. and the Staff Manual respectively. Title pages will be prepared in manuscript.

Place	Date	Hour	Summary of Events and Information	Remarks and references to Appendices
N32 a 5.9	June 3/6		In the early hours of the morning "B" Battery R.H.A. went elsewhere and handed over to A/49 their wagon line T1 b 2.4.	Ref. Map (B Sheet) Sheet 28 JW 1:20000
			Positions Battery T 2 b 8.6 Wagon Line. T 1 b 2.4. O.P. KEMMEL HILL (LITTLE) N 26 c (BLOKE ROW) Battery Hqs. N 32 a 5.9	
			Started registering the guns which extends from WULVERGHEM — MESSINES road. O 2 a 5.10. on the left to SPANBROEK MOLEN (N 30 c 2.8.) on the left Fired 2 Shrapnel and 4 lyddite	
N32 a 5.9	Fri 4/6	9 pm	Fired 2 Shrapnel and 7 lyddite.	
N32 a 5.9	Sat 5/6		Fired 8 Shrapnel and 4 lyddite. During the night the 49th Brigade (less B/49) was attached to the 46th North Midland (T.F.) Division – nearly in toto tum	

WAR DIARY
INTELLIGENCE SUMMARY
(Erase heading not required.)

Army Form C. 2118

Instructions regarding War Diaries and Intelligence Summaries are contained in F. S. Regs., Part II. and the Staff Manual respectively. Title pages will be prepared in manuscript.

Place	Date	Hour	Summary of Events and Information	Remarks and references to Appendices
N32 a 5.9	Sun 6/6		Nothing to record	Ref Map. 13 Series Sheet 28 S.W. 1:20,000
N32 a 5.9	Mon 7/6		Fired 3 Shrapnel and 7 Lyddite. Misty for observation.	PSCC-f
N32 a 5.9	Tues 8/6		Thunder storms. Fired 17 Shrapnel.	PSCC f
N32 a 5.9	Wed 9/6		Thunder showers – greatly relieved the atmosphere. The battery was paid.	PSCC f
N32 a 5.9	Thurs 10/6		Much rain during the previous night. Fired 6 Shrapnel & 3 Lyddite	PSCC g
N32 a 5.9	Fri 11/6		Fine but cool. Fired 22 Shrapnel & 5 Lyddite.	PSCC f
N32 a 5.9	Sat 12/6		Fired 2 Shrapnel & 9 Lyddite.	
N32 a 5.9	Sun 13/6		Fired 3 Lyddite. – Dull for observation	PSCC g
N32 a 5.9	Mon 14/6		Fired 9 Shrapnel – Fine	PSCC g

WAR DIARY
INTELLIGENCE SUMMARY.
(Erase heading not required.)

Army Form C. 2118

Instructions regarding War Diaries and Intelligence Summaries are contained in F. S. Regs., Part II. and the Staff Manual respectively. Title pages will be prepared in manuscript.

Place	Date	Hour	Summary of Events and Information	Remarks and references to Appendices
N32 a 5 9	Tues 15/6		Fired 13 shrapnel + 3 lyddite	Ref Map 13 series Sheet 28 SW 1:25000
N32 a 5 9	Wed 16/6	5am	Attack at HOOGE. About 5 am we fired 4 lyddite at SPANBROEK CABARET. (N30 c 37). Total number of rounds fired during the day was 3 shrapnel + 12 lyd.	
N32 a 5 9	7/6 am 17/6		Fired 8 shrapnel. At night the guns withdrew to the wagon line T.1.b.2.6. Arrangements have been made for taking over the guns (128 Heavy Arty) at the position of B/49 near VIERSTRAAT (N10 a 2.8) A/49 are no longer to belong to the 4th Div. in 6th Division but is to become the heavy battery of the 28th Division	
N3d 5.9	18/6		At night the battery took over B/49 position near VIERSTRAAT at N10 a 2.8. The guns in the position were those of the 128th (Heavy) Battery; these were left undisturbed. The following arrangements were made.	

Army Form C. 2118

WAR DIARY
INTELLIGENCE SUMMARY.
(Erase heading not required).

Instructions regarding War Diaries and Intelligence Summaries are contained in F. S. Regs., Part II. and the Staff Manual respectively. Title pages will be prepared in manuscript.

Place	Date	Hour	Summary of Events and Information	Remarks and references to Appendices
N3d 5.9.	18/6/16		A/149 handed over to B/149 - 4 guns, and 6 wagons. A/149 therefore consisted of 4 guns of the 128th (How) Battery, 2 wagons of A/149, 6 wagons of the 128th, 4 gun limbers of A/149. The following are gun positions: Battery N 10 a 2.8. Wagon Line N 1 c 9.8 Battery H.Qrs N 3 d 6.8 Gun Billet for section off duty N 3 & 5.2 Observation Billet N 6 a 6.1	Ref. Map. 13 Series. Sheet 28. S.W. 1:20,000 (PSEC) A/149 (PSEC) (PSCG)
N3d 5.9.			Owing to the considerable extent of the zone, which is the whole divisional front from MAEDELSTEDE FARM (N 24 c 9.5) on the right to the MOUND of ST ELOI (N 2d 2-8) on the left, many O P's have to be employed. The following are the principal O P's House in VIERSTRAAT (N 11 c 9.10). for right portion H ouse approximately (N 5 a 7.8) for left portion	

Army Form C. 2118

WAR DIARY
INTELLIGENCE SUMMARY
(Erase heading not required.)

Instructions regarding War Diaries and Intelligence Summaries are contained in F.S. Regs., Part II. and the Staff Manual respectively. Title pages will be prepared in manuscript.

Place	Date	Hour	Summary of Events and Information	Remarks and references to Appendices
N31 5 9	Sat 19/6/16		During the registration of the guns, some half dozen O.P.s were employed – from each of which one particular target or extent of trench could be seen. Once registered however the almost whole fire could be served from the O.P.s N.H.C 9.10 and M 3 a 7.8.	Ref map 28 Sonne Sheet 28 S.W. 1-20,000
N31 5 9	Sun 20/6		Started to register our guns. Fired to shrapnel & 11 lyddite at guns extends from Mouslehede Farm (N24 c 1.5) on far right to the Mound at St ELOI (O2 d 2.8) on the left. (sec)	
N31 5 9	Mon 21/6		Fired 5 shrapnel & 4 lyddite. 89214 Sgt HAWKINS, W. recvd to Corporal at his own request	
N31 5 9	Tue 22/6		Fired 15 shrapnel & 2 lyddite	(sec)
N31 5 9	Wed 23/6		Fired 5 shrapnel.	

Army Form C. 2118

WAR DIARY
~~INTELLIGENCE SUMMARY~~
(Erase heading not required.)

Instructions regarding War Diaries and Intelligence Summaries are contained in F. S. Regs., Part II. and the Staff Manual respectively. Title pages will be prepared in manuscript.

Place	Date	Hour	Summary of Events and Information	Remarks and references to Appendices
N 3 d 5 9	Thurs 24/6		Fired 5 Shrapnel + 9 hydolite	Ref Map 13 Series Sheet 28 S.W. 1 : 20,000
N 3 d 5 9	Fri 25/6		Fired 7 Shrapnel. Cloudy + unsettled day — some rain.	
N 3 d 5 9	Sat 26/6		Fired 19 Shrapnel + 7 hydolite. Paid the battery	
N 3 d 5 9	Sun 27/6		Fired 1 Shrapnel + 5 hydolite. Barometer 29.9	
N 3 d 5 9	Mon 28/6		Dull + cloudy. Barometer 29.0	
N 3 d 5 9	Tues 29/6		Some showers. Fired 13 Shrapnel + 3 hydolite. Barometer 29.6. Aeroplane shot in the evening.	
N 3 d 5 9	Wed 30/6		Fine and excellent light for observation. Fired 3 Shrapnel + 10 hydolite. Registered 4 targets in the evening with the aid of aeroplane observation. Barometer 29.6.	

WAR DIARY
INTELLIGENCE SUMMARY.

(Erase heading not required.)

Army Form C. 2118

Instructions regarding War Diaries and Intelligence Summaries are contained in F. S. Regs., Part II. and the Staff Manual respectively. Title pages will be prepared in manuscript.

Place	Date	Hour	Summary of Events and Information	Remarks and references to Appendices
N 3 d 5 9	9th 11/7		Issued 18 Shrapnel Barometer 32.0 PSC(?)	Ref. Map B Series Sheet 28 SW 1:20,000
N 3 d 5 9	7th 2/7		Copy of message received from B.H.R.A. 28th Division. (1) Certain indications point to the probability of a strong effort being made by the enemy against the Ypres Salient in the near future. (2) As any falling back of any part of the line would probably entail a readjustment of the front at so important that every effort should be made to prepare the gun positions for barrage switch & subsidiary lines for occupation. (3) Where Brigade Commanders are thoroughly dissatisfied with the positions prepared, steps should be taken without delay to alter or prepare others. (4) The number of trees which must be felled will be reported at once that permission may be obtained for carrying out the work. The probable times required will also be stated. (5) Now that the fronts of each Brigade have been communicated to 31st Bde. and the 3rd Bde. will continue to cover the front of Bde. the 83rd Bde. gun fronts of each line the sub-division of O.P.s should be arranged out. Infantry Bdes. sgnd V.M Ferguson B.M.R.A	

Army Form C. 2118

WAR DIARY
INTELLIGENCE SUMMARY.
(Erase heading not required.)

Instructions regarding War Diaries and Intelligence Summaries are contained in F. S. Regs., Part II. and the Staff Manual respectively. Title pages will be prepared in manuscript.

Place	Date	Hour	Summary of Events and Information	Remarks and references to Appendices
N 3 d 5.9	Fri 2/7		Fired 14 Shrapnel. Barometer 30.2.	Ref. Map 1/8 Series. Sheet 28 SW 1:20000
N 3 d 5.9	Sat 3/7		Fired 1 Shrapnel + 2 Lyddite. Barometer 30.2.	PSC CJ
N 3 d 5.9	Sun 4/7		Fired 4 Shrapnel 9 Lyddite. Barometer 30.	PSC CJ
N 3 d 5.9	Mon 5/7		Fired 8 Shrapnel. Dull for observation. Barometer 29.9.	PSC CJ
N 3 d 5.9	Tues 6/7		Did not fire. Barometer 30.	
N 3 d 5.9	Wed 7/7		Dull + cold. Fired 15 Shrapnel + 2 Lyddite. Barometer 29.7	PSC CJ
N 3 d 5.9	Thurs 8/7		Fired 9 Shrapnel + 3 Lyddite. Barometer 29.8	

13

Army Form C. 2118

WAR DIARY
or
INTELLIGENCE SUMMARY.
(Erase heading not required.)

Instructions regarding War Diaries and Intelligence
Summaries are contained in F. S. Regs., Part II.
and the Staff Manual respectively. Title pages
will be prepared in manuscript.

Place	Date	Hour	Summary of Events and Information	Remarks and references to Appendices
N3d5.9	Fri 9/7/17		Some rain	Ref Map B Series Sheet 28 JW 1:20,000
N3d5.9	Sat 10/7		Fired 22 Shrapnel & 15 Lyddite. Barometer 30.1	PSCCJ
			Readjustment of Infantry Brigade fronts is ordered – PSCCJ	
			83rd Bde. G1 to K2 Both inclusive	
			84th Bde. K2 to N5 Both inclusive	
			85th Bde. N5 to present left	
N3d0.9				
N3d5.9	Sun 11/7		Showery. Fired 8 Shrapnel & 6 Lyddite Barometer 29.9	PSCCJ
N3d5.9	Mon 12/7		Showery. Fired 4 Shrapnel & 3 Lyddite. Barometer 28.5	
			On the night 12/13th the 22nd Division took over from the 50th Divn the front line trenches up to and including the KEMMEL – WYTSCHAETE ROAD.	
N3d5.9	Tues 13/7		Paid the battery	
			Barometer 29.8	PSCCJ

WAR DIARY
INTELLIGENCE SUMMARY.
(Erase heading not required.)

Army Form C. 2118

Place	Date	Hour	Summary of Events and Information	Remarks and references to Appendices
N 3 d 5.9	Wed 14/7		Shrapnel and Lyddite fired. Barometer 28.5. Copy of 28th Divisional Artillery Operation Order No.10.	Ref Map B Sevex Sheet 28 SW 1:20000

1. The 27th, & 28th Brigades, R.F.A, will relieve the 146th and 31st Bdes R.F.A respectively.

2. Reliefs will be carried out a section at a time, as usual. The front section will be relieved on the night of 16/17 July. Relieving sections will take over from the 1st & 2nd Northumbrian Bdes respectively the same night.

3. 31st Bde Sections will be withdrawn by 7.30 pm and will march via X Rds N10 & 8.5; N10 a; N16 a to road junction N16 a 4.7, where they will be met by guides of the 2nd Northumbrian Brigade.

4. 146th Bde Sections will be withdrawn by 7.30 pm and will march via LA CLYTTE — LOCRE — DRANOUTRE to Church DRANOUTRE, where they will be met by guides.

All reliefs will be reported to this Office when complete.

WAR DIARY
INTELLIGENCE SUMMARY
(Erase heading not required.)

Army Form C. 2118

Place	Date	Hour	Summary of Events and Information	Remarks and references to Appendices
Maytros N3 & 5 & 9	Wed 14/7 cont.		5. Officers commanding Brigades will continue to hold their commands until 12 noon 17-7-15, at which time all registration of incoming sections should be complete.	Ref. Maps B Series Sheet 28 S.W. 1:20,000
			At 12 noon 17-7-15 all communications and command will be handed over to the incoming C.O.s. Command will be taken over from the Northern Group Posts at 6 p.m.	
			6. On the night of 17/18 July the remaining sections will be relieved and in turn will relieve the remaining sections of the Northern Group Bdes.	
			7. The A/49 th Howitzer Battery will be relieved by the 63 th (How.) Battery (less one section), but "B" in all probability will exchange positions. Further orders will be issued on this subject. The first section of A/49 Howt. Battery will move to its new position on the night of 16/17 July. The relief being completed the following night.	
			Note. Ammunition should be based as far as possible for the new two days. Signed V R Brinkhurst Staff Capt R.A. Ft 2	

Army Form C. 211

WAR DIARY
INTELLIGENCE SUMMARY.
(Erase heading not required.)

Place	Date	Hour	Summary of Events and Information	Remarks and references to Appendices
Dickebusch	15/7		Preparations for taking over and handing over to the 65th Howitzer Battery R.F.A.	Ref Map B series Sheet 28 SW 1: 20,000.
Verstraat N3 d 5 9			Arrangements were made that the Battery should take over 3 guns of the 65th Battery - also 6 wagons. The remainder of the vehicles of the Battery consisted of one gun (originally (28pr.)) and 2 wagons + 4 gun limbers of A/49's own.	
Dickebusch			2/Lt. P. R. Hughes admitted to hospital. — 2/Lt. H. Culpin was sent from the 3rd Brigade Ammunition Column and attached to the battery.	
Verstraat N3 d 5 9	16/7	6.30 pm	65th Battery (Howitzer 4.5") (Major D. G. Peters) took over the battery's position etc. The right section and B.A.C. (attached) withdrew from action about 6.30pm and proceeded to new wagon line T 2 c 4.8	
		9.30 pm	The left section withdrew from action about 9.30 pm and proceeded to new wagon line M 24 d 10.5.	

WAR DIARY
INTELLIGENCE SUMMARY

Army Form C. 211

Instructions regarding War Diaries and Intelligence Summaries are contained in F. S. Regs., Part II. and the Staff Manual respectively. Title pages will be prepared in manuscript.

(Erase heading not required.)

Summary of Events and Information from 28th D.A.C.

Place	Date	Hour	Summary of Events and Information	Remarks and references to Appendices
M34 d10.5	Sat 17/7		202. A/Bty OSBORNE. E. Battery at rest in wagon lines during day. The Right section and one section of the 49th Bde Ammunition Column (attached) were at T 2 c 4 8. The Left section was at M 24 d 10.5. At dusk the battery went in action. Right section took over the position of the 4th Durham (How.) Battery of the 4th Northumbrian (County of Durham) (Howitzer) Brigade 50th Div. [T 3 & 5.6] Left Section took over the position of the 3th Durham (How.) Battery of the 4th Northumbrian (County of Durham) (Howitzer) Brigade. 50th Div [M 15 & 2 7] Fired 14 Shrapnel and air lyddite.	Ref Map B Series Sheet 28. S.W. 1: 20,000
M24 d 10.5	Sun 18/7		Started to register new zone extends from Ruins (N 36 d 6 2) on the right to X Rds (N 18 b 7 2) on the left. Battery Headquarters and left section wagon line (M 24 d 10.5) Right Section wagon line and Ammunition Column (attached) T 2 c 4 8 Observation Station – Dug out near KEMMEL TOWER	

WAR DIARY or INTELLIGENCE SUMMARY.

Army Form C. 2118.

(Erase heading not required.)

Instructions regarding War Diaries and Intelligence Summaries are contained in F. S. Regs., Part II. and the Staff Manual respectively. Title pages will be prepared in manuscript.

Place	Date	Hour	Summary of Events and Information	Remarks and references to Appendices
M.24.d.10.5	Mon 19/7 1917		Fired – 29 Shrapnel and 15 Lyddite. Secret Points of Junction between Poles and Div ns on lines of Defence.	Ref. Map. B Series Sheet 28 SW
			Line: Between Canadian Div & 85th Bde. / Between 85th & 84th Bdes / Between 84th & 83rd Bdes / Between 83rd Bde & 5th Div:	
			U.i.a.3.2 (Trench Connaughan) / N.30.c (E.1 & E.6 of 85th Bde) / N.24.a (H.4 and L.6 of 84th Bde) / VIERSTRAAT – WYTSCHAETE Road and to 5th Div.	
			Front Line: 143 to 85th (Connaughan)	1:20,000.
			Exact points of junction to be fixed between Brigade Commanders.	
			PSC C/9	
M.24.d.16.5	Tues 20/7		Fine day. Total number of rounds fired 31 Shrapnel and 4 Lyddite. Ammunition for week increased to 200 Shrapnel. 100 Lyddite.	PSC C/9
M.24.d.10.5	Wed 21/7		Fine day with much sun. Total number of rounds fired during day – 25 Shrapnel and 13 Lyddite. 88945 Dvr. Henderson S. appointed Shoeing Smith. 31379 Sgt POOLE, J. was posted to battery	

WAR DIARY
INTELLIGENCE SUMMARY.

Army Form C. 2118

Instructions regarding War Diaries and Intelligence Summaries are contained in F. S. Regs., Part II. and the Staff Manual respectively. Title pages will be prepared in manuscript.

(Erase heading not required.)

Place	Date	Hour	Summary of Events and Information	Remarks and references to Appendices
M24 d 10.5	Thurs 22/7		Showery. Total number of rounds fired during the day — 20 Shrapnel and 13 Lyddite. Cpl Sherry Smith & Sherwood G has posted to the battery from 4A40, 21st reserve battery R.F.A. (PSC<J)	Map. B Jones Sheet 28 SW 1:20,000
M24 d 10.5	Fri 23/7		Showery. Total number of rounds fired during day — 20 Shrapnel and 21 Lyddite. (PSC<J)	
M24 d 10.5	Sat 24/7		Fair to moderate. Some showers. Total number of rounds fired during the day was 38 Shrapnel and 24 Lyddite.	
		3pm.	As an experiment two targets were registered by means of Balloon Observation. Fair results obtained. (PSC<J)	

WAR DIARY

INTELLIGENCE SUMMARY.

(Erase heading not required.)

Army Form C. 2118

Place	Date	Hour	Summary of Events and Information	Remarks and references to Appendices
M24 d10.5	1915 25/7		Showery and thundery. Barometer 29.5. Fired during day 29 Shrapnel and 4 Lyddite. 2/Bdr WILKINSON J. reverted to Driver & O for Wetherose.	Map "B" Series Sheet 28 SW 1:20000
M24 d10.5	Mon 26/7		Unsettled. Barometer 29.8. Fired 20 Shrapnel & 13 Lyddite. 27081 2/c/Bdr ATKINSON. D. posted to 28th D.A.C.	
M24 d10.5	Tues 27/7		Fair. Some showers — Barometer 29.82 — Fired 14 Lyddite	
M24 d10.5	Wed 28/7		Fine. Barometer 30.04. Fired 4 Shrapnel and 11 Lyddite Paid the battery. Secret. 28th Division wire begun. "Following relief took place last night. 84th Bde relieved 83rd Bde in H 5 and the 7th trenches and in SP 12. Following relief takes place tonight. 85th Bde relieves 84th Bde in E2 trench. For your information. — Batteries will continue to the present to cover their allotted zones but the 365th Battery is temporarily placed under the tactical control of Major H.H. Bond commanding 31st Bde R.F.A. The O.C. 3rd & 31st Bde will arrange for suitable communications to be established 3rd V.H. Fergusson, Major BMRA.	

WAR DIARY

INTELLIGENCE SUMMARY.

(Erase heading not required.)

Army Form C. 2118

Instructions regarding War Diaries and Intelligence Summaries are contained in F. S. Regs., Part II. and the Staff Manual respectively. Title pages will be prepared in manuscript.

Place	Date	Hour	Summary of Events and Information	Remarks and references to Appendices
N24.d.10.5	Wed 28/7 (cont)		Sent to O.C A/49. (1) At 3.30 pm tomorrow (29th) a combined shoot is being undertaken on the HOSPICE (O.19.a.8.8.) (2) The 3rd Div's Heavy Guns and some of the 3rd Group H.A.R. will also be shooting (3) You will participate in this to the extent of 10 rounds of Lyddite (4) Watches will be set during the morning (5) Ammunition 28/7/15 } Fuze 6.5 pm } V.H. Tompson Major BMRA.	Ref Map B Series Sheet 28 SW 1:20,000
M.24.d.10.5	Thurs 29/7	3.30 pm	Barometer 30.15 . Fine Battery participated in a shoot against HOSPICE (O.19 a.8.8) to the extent of 10 rounds of Lyddite Result the enemy immediately started putting heavy shells into KEMMEL Village	

Army Form C. 2118

WAR DIARY
INTELLIGENCE SUMMARY.
(Erase heading not required.)

Place	Date	Hour	Summary of Events and Information	Remarks and references to Appendices
M24d10.5	Shurt 29/7 (cont)	3.30 p.m.	Statement from CRA – 9gned VM Ferguson Major BMRA 28th Div". At 3.30 pm. this afternoon the 21st Siege Battery, in cooperation with the 3rd Divisional Artillery, attempted to destroy the HOSPICE (O19a 8.8). The building itself was not actually hit direct. The Germans replied with 5·9" Shrapnel and 8·2" HE on KEMMEL.	Ref. Map B Series Sheet 28 SW. 1-20,000
M24d 10·5	30/7	7a.	Fine – misty at times. Barometer 30·14". Fired 9 Shrapnel + 22 Lyd.	
"	Sat 31/7		Fine – Barometer 30". Fired 15 Lyddite	
"	Sun Aug 1st	9 am to 10 am	Fine - Barometer 29·84". Slight SW breeze. Fired 11 Lyddite + 3 Sh? The left section at N.15 b 2.7. were shelled with 5·9" HE. Observation carried out by hostile observation balloon about 16 in all. No damage + no casualties.	P.7/8
"			+ aeroplane – The right section wagon line + B.A.C. (attached) moved from T.2 d 3·3 to T.2 d 3·3. Cpl Pearce C.H. from 14 & A.A. Section.	

WAR DIARY
INTELLIGENCE SUMMARY.

(Erase heading not required.)

Army Form C. 2118

24

Place	Date	Hour	Summary of Events and Information	Remarks and references to Appendices
N 24 d 10.5 7.1b.	Sat 7/8		The demonstration on SPANBROEK MOLEN (N 30 a 2.8) was postponed for 24 hours. Fired 8 Shrapnel during the day. Battery headquarters & left section wagon lines were moved to the right section wagon T 2 d 3.3. BURGRAVE FARM (M 24 d 10.5) became the headquarters of the 3rd Bde R.F.A. The battery became the howitzer battery of the 146th Bde R.F.A. (Major P.P.E. de Berry). The left section at N 22 a 2.7 was moved to the position of the right section at T 3 & 6.8, hence the battery became together.	Ref Map B. Series. Sheet 28. S.W. 1 : 20,000
T 2 d 3.3	Sun 8/8		The B.A.C. (attached) under 2/Lt. C.H.L. Penney left for the 146th B.A.C. 3 officers — Major R.A. Mc'Clymont, 2/Lt. E.D. Carruthers and 2/Lieut G. Holmes — and 27 NCO's and men of 13/126.	

Army Form C. 211

WAR DIARY
INTELLIGENCE SUMMARY.
(Erase heading not required.)

Place	Date	Hour	Summary of Events and Information	Remarks and references to Appendices
T2 d 3.3.	Sun 8/8 (cont)		Pte. R.F.A.) 37th Division came to the battery for a week's instruction. Fired 19 Shrapnel and 4 Lyddite	Ref Map 10 series Sheet 28 SW 1:20000
T2 d 3.3.	Mon 9/8		During the attack on the trenches (lost on July 30th, due to the enemy's use of flame projectors) in the region of HOOGE, the battery demonstrated for thirty minutes on SPANBROEK MOLEN (N 30 c 2.8). A German stronghold on the battery's front.	
		3 am	Between 3 am – 3·10 am 10 Lyddite were fired. Between 3·20 am – 3·40 am 74 Shrapnel & 30 Lyddite were fired. making a grand total of 74 shrapnel & 40 Lyddite. At 4 am 18 pdr batteries and one 9.2 howitzer co-operated. The wagon line was moved to T 2 c 4.8. In order to silence an enemy "Minenwerfer", the battery fired	
		10 pm	12 Lyddite at the request of the infantry between 9.30 pm & 10.30 pm. This particular mortar taken by the enemy was of considerable	

26/

Army Form C. 21

WAR DIARY
INTELLIGENCE SUMMARY.
(Erase heading not required.)

Instructions regarding War Diaries and Intelligence Summaries are contained in F. S. Regs., Part II. and the Staff Manual respectively. Title pages will be prepared in manuscript.

Place	Date	Hour	Summary of Events and Information	Remarks and references to Appendices
T5 a 3.8.	Mon 9/8 (cont)		siege and caused damage in D4 trench. Total rounds fired during the day — 74 shrapnel + 52 lyddite	Ref. Maps. 1/5 Series Sheet 28 SW 1:20000
T3 a 3.8	Tues 10/8		Various positions:— Battery. T 3 & 6. 8. Wagon line. T 2 c 4. 8. Headquarters T 3 a 3 8. Fired 15 shrapnel + 5 lyddite.	PSCC?
T3 a 3.8	Wed 11/8		Fine. Fired 4 shrapnel	PSCC?
T3a 3.8	Thurs 12/8		Excellent for observation. Fired 6 shrapnel.	
T3 a 3.8	Fri 13/8		Fine and warm. Fired 1 shrapnel + 20 lyddite. The battery was found	
T3a 3.8	Sat 14/8		Excellent for observation and aviation — fine and warm — light breeze. Fired 8 shrapnel.	PSCC?
T3 a 3.8	Sun 15/8		The 3 officers and 27 NCOs + men at 13/126, 37th Division returned to their own unit. Fired 9 shrapnel	PSCC?

WAR DIARY
INTELLIGENCE SUMMARY.
(Erase heading not required.)

Army Form C. 21.

Instructions regarding War Diaries and Intelligence Summaries are contained in F. S. Regs., Part II. and the Staff Manual respectively. Title pages will be prepared in manuscript.

Place	Date	Hour	Summary of Events and Information	Remarks and references to Appendices
T3 a 3.8	Mon 16/8		Very misty for observation. Fired 4 Shrapnel. Thundery.	Ref Map 1:B Series Sheet 28 SW 1:20,000. PSCC ?
T3 a 3.8	Tues 17/8		Heavy thunder storm about noon. Fired 4 Shrapnel & 2 hydulite. 53372 Saddler LOVELESS. E.J. from 66th Bty RFA SW	
T3 a 3.8	Wed 18/8		Fine. Test in the after noon. Fired 14 Shrapnel	(PSCC?)
T3 a 3.8	Thurs 19/8		Fine. Fired 10 Shrapnel + 12 hyddite	PSCC?
T3 a 3.8	Fri 20/8		Fine. Fired 12 Shrapnel	
T3 a 3.8	Sat 21/8		Cold – wind in the north. Fired 8 shrapnel + 3 hyddite. Light excellent for observation.	(PSCC?)
T3 a 3.8	Sun 22/8			
T3 a 3.8	Mon 23/8		Major G. H. Bridge – Cowaly A/49 – went on leave to England. 89160 Bdr Tittle. A.C. and 10837 Gunner Morton W. were wounded in the trenches the former in the neck & neck, the latter above the right knee. Cause. Explosion of one of our own bombs.	257

WAR DIARY
INTELLIGENCE SUMMARY.
(Erase heading not required.)

Army Form C. 2118

Place	Date	Hour	Summary of Events and Information	Remarks and references to Appendices
T3 a 3.8	Tues 24/8		Fired 10 Shrapnel + 2 Lyddite. Fine.	Ref Map B Series Sheet 28 SW 1: 20,000
T3 a 3.8	Wed 25/8		Too misty for observation purposes. Fine. 202 Pte a/Bdr OSBORNE, E. promoted Bdr + posted to 367th Bty. Thurs	
T3 a 3.8	26/8		4/8191 Gunner BRIGHTWELL, promoted a/Bdr + posted to A/149. Fired 13 Shrapnel + 1 Lyddite. from Hy. 146 Bde. R.F.A.	
T3 a 3.8	Fri 27/8		Fine. Fired 4 Shrapnel. The enemy sent about a dozen salvoes of 10.5 cm shells between the battery + the battery hqs (T 3 b 6.8) - no casualties.	(PSCC)
T3 a 3.8	Sat 28/8	10 pm	Fine - excellent for observation. Between 10 pm + 10.20 pm from the battery fired several rounds at hostile transport moving along the MESSINES - WYTSCHAETE road towards MESSINES. Fired 6 Sht and 15 Lyddite during the twenty four hours.	
T3 a 3.8	Sun 29/8		Major A. H. BRIDGES returned from leave. Lt-Col K.P.G. de BERRY sent on leave and Major A.H. BRIDGES became acting/OC 146 Bde R.F.A. Wet.	

WAR DIARY
or
INTELLIGENCE SUMMARY.

(Erase heading not required.)

Army Form C. 2118.

Instructions regarding War Diaries and Intelligence Summaries are contained in F. S. Regs., Part II. and the Staff Manual respectively. Title pages will be prepared in manuscript.

Place	Date	Hour	Summary of Events and Information	Remarks and references to Appendices
T3 a 3.8	Mon 30/8		Fine but dull and bad for observation. Two 10.5 cm shells fell within twenty-five yards of the guns. No casualties.	Ref Map 1:40 Series Sheet 28 SW 1:20000
T3 a 3.8	Tues 31/8		The battery was found. Sgt POOLE, G.31377, sent on course owing to the fact that forms with cordite charges had been mistaken; the battery tested various makes – V.S.M. – R.L – K.7. one against the other and compared them with ballistic charges.	
T3 a 3.8	Wed Sept 1st		Fired 7 Shrapnel and 4 Lyddite. Bad light for observation. Wet. 1441 Driver Sergeant DAVEY, T promoted Staff Sergeant-turner	
T3 a 3.8.	2/9 Thurs 7/n		Cloudy – cold – some rain. Fired 5 Shrapnel and 8 Lyddite.	
T3 a 3.8.	3/9		Very wet. It rained throughout the day. The ammunition column sections of A/49, A/73 & 13/89 respectively are formed into a Brigade Ammunition Column at M 32 & 5.6	P.S.C.C.f

1014/121

38th Division

"B"/130 Battery R.F.A. (late B/89 Battery)

Vol III

Sept 15

Army Form C. 2118

WAR DIARY
or
INTELLIGENCE SUMMARY
(Erase heading not required.)

B Battery 89th Brigade RFA

Unit 130th

Place	Date	Hour	Summary of Events and Information	Remarks and references to Appendices
LANDENHOEK	1 Sept 1915	8.45 pm	Fired 6 rounds of lyddite in retaliation at 10.30 pm at SPANBROEK MOLEN. G.2 Howitzer Bty shelled PECKHAM between 5.0 & 6.30 pm. Enemy retaliated with some heavy shell but as usual well behind the trenches & did harm less. Commenced a dugout in right of Battery, about 8 pieces of iron sheeting received. Gun emplacements further strengthened with sandbags. DWG	
LANDENHOEK	2 Sept 1915	9.20 pm	Barometer 29.45. Much rain. CRA inspected the battery position at 9.45 am. 10 pm fired 6 rounds lyddite at SPANBROEK MOLEN in retaliation. Commenced to alter No.2 Gun Emplacement & No.2 to bring the gun further forward into the body of the pit in front - having dried up. Cut trench irrigating channels to carry off storm water from No.2 Gun Position. DWG	
LANDENHOEK	3 Sept 1915	9.6 pm	Barometer 29.43. Much rain all day. Gun position very sodden. Did not fire. Guns loaded with — by Forth Corner last night. Enemy fired 6 TMs on PECKHAM firing cancelled — enemy has exploded mine in G.2 Inf Battery came of it.	
LANDENHOEK	4 Sept 1915	7.10 pm	Between 1.30 & 2.0 pm fired zero rounds by Bde in retaliation on SPANBROEK MOLEN & and at 2.35 pm 2 rounds on PECKHAM, who at 5.30 pm are winked on MAEDELSTEDE. Major Gun CAREY to Command the 130th Bde. RFA visited the battery at 5.0 pm. The 130th Bde will command 9 Aug, A73 & B89 Batteries. The BAC Subaltern & each battery concentrated yesterday at M.35.c 5.6. By orders the 130 & 84 Ammunition Columns. DWG	

1875 Wt. W503/826 1,000,000 4/15 J.B.C. & A. A.D.S.S./Forms/C. 2118.

WAR DIARY
or
INTELLIGENCE SUMMARY
(Erase heading not required.)

Army Form C. 2118

B Battery 88 Brigade RFA

Place	Date	Hour	Summary of Events and Information	Remarks and references to Appendices
LANDENHOEK	Sept 5	9.30 pm	Bombdt 30.03 Ammunition 11.25 am fired two effective rounds of Lyddite into the BLACK REDOUBT. 11.35 am Registered left section on L'ENFER ENTRENCHMENTS and at 12.30 pm six SAP in front of MAEDELSTEDE. 5.15 pm fired six rounds of Shrapnel at L'ENFER with balloon observation. 6.0 pm fired four Lyddite at BLACK REDOUBT. Were effective. E.A.B.	
LANDENHOEK	6 Sept	9.0 pm	Bombdt 30.23 Fine morning. 5.30 pm fired 8 rounds at BLACK REDOUBT. 118 Bty Cooperating with Shrapnel after each round 7 H.E. Cordite used at first but very impracticable. Six rounds fired 200" short + not far from our trenches. Afternoon Lyddite with very accurate shooting. Saw also that Cordite was never to be used for trench work + only when charge 5 was required at midday. Enemy put in 4 H.E. in 366-157 in front 2 in Kemmel 4 Shrapnel 200" further back on our right, fragments 75 lb. Came into our Battery. E.A.B.	
LANDENHOEK	7 Sept	9.0 pm	Fired 3 Lyddite + 3 Shrapnel at BLACK REDOUBT at 3.30 pm, 118 Battery cooperating. All Lyddite were effective. Ranging rifle with 3 "Crumps" behind 76 Stewart. Aeroplane came over at 11.0 am Taguin at 5.30, each time getting a considerable distance to our rear.	

WAR DIARY
or
INTELLIGENCE SUMMARY

(Erase heading not required.)

Army Form C. 2118

B Battery 130th Brigade R.F.A.

Place	Date	Hour	Summary of Events and Information	Remarks and references to Appendices
LANDENHOEK	8/9/15	4.0 pm	Barrels 30 Rds - Fuze Timer. Today on authority A.G., G.H.Q., No.A.Q./D/123 dated 3.9.15 the Battery designation altered to B/130th Brigade R.F.A. The following three Batteries are now brigaded together:— A Battery 49th Brigade becomes A Battery 130th Brigade / B " 89 " " B " " / C " 73 " " C " " / No 2 Gun's new position being completed, registered the gun & took on reference lines at 2.30 pm. Fired 2 hy shell + 2 Shrapnel at the BLACK REDOUBT at 3.30 pm. 115 Battery co-operating - 1 hy shell & shrapnel effective.	SWS
LANDENHOEK	9/9/15	7.45 / 10 pm	Barrels 30.12. 2nd Operation order 31st Brigade No 26 dated 2/9/9/15. Fired 5 hy shells at BLACK REDOUBT at 5.15 pm. 115th By & 100 Battery co-operating. 2 rounds direct hit on parapet, carried away a considerable portion. Whole subsequent rounds severely damages the further side of the Redoubt. Splinter front ridge in each gun pit running completion	SWS IV
LANDENHOEK	10/9/15	6.10 pm	Fired 2 hy shells + 2 Shrapnel at BLACK REDOUBT at 4.0 pm. all effective. German had been seen running in parapet but very little attention been _____ to the damage of yesterday	SWS

WAR DIARY
or
INTELLIGENCE SUMMARY
(Erase heading not required.)

Army Form C. 2118

Instructions regarding War Diaries and Intelligence Summaries are contained in F. S. Regs., Part II. and the Staff Manual respectively. Title Pages will be prepared in manuscript.

Place	Date	Hour	Summary of Events and Information	Remarks and references to Appendices
LANDENHOEK	11/9/16	6.30 pm	Bombli. 30.07. Fired at BLACK REDOUBT at 3.30 pm, 118 Btg cooperating – 34 Shells + 2 Shrapnel; all effect ins, 2 H.E. were direct hits and carried away large portion of the Earthwork; some rebuilding had been done during the night. 20 Shrapnel fell in trench filed emptg. Walking at 4.30 pm. EWS	
LANDENHOEK	12/9/15	7 pm	Bombli. 29.97. very warm. Fired 2 rounds 6 lyddite at SPANBROEK MOLEN at 10.05 am. At 11.45 am our 9 in. Howg. lyddite has burst in BLACK REDOUBT which 2nd Lt LUMSDEN observed from Trench G 2. It is certain the exact point of the REDOUBT for exact. Captain 9. 4.0 pm Quadrilaterals NO 27, 312 Angouls R.F.A. Appendix V – Fired 3 R Lyddite at BLACK REDOUBT from Battery cooperating L'MUDIE in charge – made an attempt at 3.20 pm to range a target with observation by the Captive Balloon but communication failed at first round. RW	V
LANDENHOEK	13/9/15	6.10 pm	Bombli. 29.84. warm. 3.0 pm fired into lyddite + two shrapnel at BLACK REDOUBT, 118 TBattery cooperating. Even of the day being overcast preventing trenches being observed to which during the explosions of the recent rounds if were – 10098. Yesterday their was no error in the range as regards. The range was very carefully regulated during the warm weather in [illegible]. EWS	

Army Form C. 2118

WAR DIARY
or
INTELLIGENCE SUMMARY
(Erase heading not required.)

Instructions regarding War Diaries and Intelligence Summaries are contained in F.S. Regs., Part II. and the Staff Manual respectively. Title Pages will be prepared in manuscript.

Place	Date	Hour	Summary of Events and Information	Remarks and references to Appendices
LANDENHOEK	14/9/15	6.40 pm	Barom. 29.74 cloudy - low warm. Windsight W S.S. 2.45 pm: fired 34 H.E. at SPANBROEK MOLEN and three 4 H.E. at BLACK REDOUBT in retaliation. 3 began fires 2 Shrapnel at BLACK REDOUBT were change 2 instead of 9 Burst # -60 ft high burst.	
LANDENHOEK	15/9/15	4.30 pm	Barom. 29.97. Fine warm. Western. 2pm 4 O'DONOVAN observed from French 2.2 a view post on Machine Gun at N.W. corner of PETIT BOIS N 24 a 7±6 Between 12.10 pm & 3.10 pm Communication very slow owing to heavy fire through 36, 135 rounds to 3rd Bde R.9.a. 6 31". Bde R.9.a. before reaching battery. Fired 9 Shrapnel 4 h hits - 6 effective.	
LANDENHOEK	16/9/15	9.45 pm	9.45 about 12 Shrapnel fell near LANDENHOEK coming from direction of LENFERS Chandlier (altn) No 2 E. 31.43 d. R.9a. counselled at 11.5 pm away from the pay post light. And very hazy. APPENDIX VI. 2/Lt LUMSDEN went to E1 Trench to observe fire on horses at N 30 c 22 ½	VI
LANDENHOEK	17/9/15	6.40 pm	Barom. 30.20. very warm. No wind. Operation order No 24. 31 Bde R.9a. carried out the afternoon - produced Aten No 2 B 9 yesterday that was cancelled. Fired 4 ranging rounds with 18 Shrapnel at N 30 a 2.35 at 4.30 a.m. & 5 Lyddite in conjunction with Aten at 4.00 pm - 4 effective with direct hit.	VII

WAR DIARY or INTELLIGENCE SUMMARY

(Erase heading not required.)

Army Form C. 2118.

Instructions regarding War Diaries and Intelligence Summaries are contained in F. S. Regs., Part II. and the Staff Manual respectively. Title Pages will be prepared in manuscript.

Place	Date	Hour	Summary of Events and Information	Remarks and references to Appendices
LANDENHOEK	19/9/15	6.15 p.m.	Barometer 30.05. Wind N.W. 7 miles per hour. Fired 5 lyddite & shrapnel in front of SPANBROEK MOLEN at 1.30 p.m. in retaliation for enemy's F2 trenches. At 4.20 a.m. by shite at MAEDESTEDE in retaliation for continued enemy gun fire not now praticed.	
SPANBROEK LANDENHOEK	19/9/15	6.30 p.m.	Barometer 30 N. Wind E.B. 8 miles per hour. Fired 3 shrapnel at 11.30 a.m. and ten lyddite between 3.40 p.m. and 4.0 p.m. at SPANBROEK MOLEN in retaliation. At 4.10 p.m. registered with 1 shrapnel & fired 6 lyddite for effect on enemy trenches opposite 15 trench. All lyddite speedwith & dreinfitch. Lieut MUDIE observed the effect from trench 15.	
LANDENHOEK	20/9/15	7.15 p.m.	Barometer 30.07. Wind E 4, N – 13 miles per hour. Fired counterbombard at rifle fire at O.25-c.9.9. – on WYTSCHAETE RIDGE – at 2.35 p.m.	
LANDENHOEK	21/9/15		Barometer 30.05. Wind NE 4, E- 7 miles per hour. Garden Actor NO.31, 31.2 pm RFA received and might transmit this position in which might be the 22-23. Artillery party went to BORRE this morning. Fired in retaliation at 3.30 pm & 6.20 pm at SPANBROEK MOLEN & mound by about in each case.	VIII
LANDENHOEK	22/9/15		Barometer 30.07. Wind ESE light. No firing today. German Aeroplane over this morning again over Battalion imaging a battery on this side of KEMMEL HILL - another found this morning coming from the direction of your rear. The German has been shelled by two 2" in shells. Balloon to N.W. was released - Preparing to transmit position at 7.30 pm cast	

WAR DIARY or INTELLIGENCE SUMMARY

Army Form C. 2118

Instructions regarding War Diaries and Intelligence Summaries are contained in F.S. Regs., Part II. and the Staff Manual respectively. Title Pages will be prepared in manuscript.

(Erase heading not required.)

Place	Date	Hour	Summary of Events and Information	Remarks and references to Appendices
BORRE	24/9/15		Evacuated our gun position at LANDENHOEK 6 to 20 pm on the night 22nd - 23rd Slept at Night time DRANOUTRE - Marched yesterday at 9.30 am thro' BAILLEUL followed by 31st Bde Rta. Route through METEREN, FLETRES, PRADELLES, Reached BORRE at 4.30 pm. Length March 12 miles. Received orders to march at an hour's notice. - Bgd engagement to commence at 6 am tomorrow, we stood at an hour's notice.	
HINGES	25/9/15 6 to 7 pm		No movement September. Information received last evening the attack has been successful in places particular SOUTH of LA BASSEE. What the truth may be seen Saturday night. Orders after No 1 13.07hr RTR 24/9/15 received at 5.45 am - Bryad marched from BORRE - The batty leaving Hd. Billet at 7.45 am - joined the rest of Bde. 20th DIVISION route through VIEUX BERQUIN, NEUF BERQUIN, MERVILLE - Battery entered new billet at 4.0 pm - Situated on the border of the CANAL D'AIRE A LA BASSEE just NORTH of HINGES. Length March 14 miles - Long the CANAL D'AIRE A LA BASSEE to the	1 X
MONT BERNENCHON	26/9/15 8.30 am		Yesterday afternoon. March down the SOUTH side of the CANAL D'AIRE A LA BASSEE to another billet	2X
MONT BERNENCHON	26/9/15 10.0 pm		2nd Bn. Gr 5.0 am proceeded via BETHUNE to ANNEQUIN with Lieut MUDIE to reconnoitre & commence taking over from 53rd Bde RFA this batty Gds Hrs from C.53.B.5.5. Arrived at ANNEQUIN at 11.0 am Left at 3.0 pm after investigating battery positions & taking over first the detachen from observation station in a slag heap (FOSSE) close to on Der G'nalle tactical situation at present uproar, enemy retiring reluctant by country. Seen not in sufficient strength + yet but to return to a great army C.53.B.5.5 with no position a slag in lort line	

1875 ¹ Wt. W5933/826 N⁴1000,000 4/15 J.B.C. & A. A.D.S.S./Forms/C. 2118.

28th Div

"B" Batty 130th Bde. RHA:
occ trons.

IV + V

28th Divn.
Army Form C. 2118

WAR DIARY
or
INTELLIGENCE SUMMARY
(Erase heading not required.)

B Battery 130th Brigade R.F.A.

Place	Date	Hour	Summary of Events and Information	Remarks and references to Appendices
ANNEQUIN	7/10/15	10.30	Yesterday received orders to relieve 034 - 53 Bde R.F.A. at 6.0 p.m. Right section went in at 3.0 p.m. last evening, relief completed by 5.0 p.m. today. Position is in old R.F.A. position. Left gun pits will protected. 12.15 a.m. battery registered right section of MADAGASCAR HOUSES in 2000 line. From 2.0 p.m. until 3.30 shelled NORTH FACE of HOHENZOLLERN REDOUBT - fired 96 Lyddite-Heavy (mechanical) shrapnel gunners captured the SOUTH FACE - fired 96 Lyddite-Heavy (mechanical) on LittleWillie Trench, began at 2.0 pm & lifted at 3.30 pm when infantry attacked LittleWillie. Every shell to now left intermittently from 4.30 pm onwards from Bde HQ but they are bombarding few shells. [sig]	
ANNEQUIN	8/10/15	9.0 am	"Little Willie" trench taken by us last night, then lost again, then taken again. Last reported left flank in Zero line (MADAGASCAR). During attack on Ruth Wyke at 3.15 pm registered TRANSVAAL with Rightsection, this proved inconvenient so over 2 Bath Willie at 3.35 pm ordered to open fire on communication trench to HOSE TRENCH, all hurt, 4.0 P. But at 5.10 pm no information forthcoming sighted guns at larger from 8.15 to 9 pm bottling bombardment of "Little Willie" in preparation for infantry attack at 9.30 pm. [sig]	

WAR DIARY
or
INTELLIGENCE SUMMARY
(Erase heading not required.)

Army Form C. 2118

B Battery 150 Brigade RFA

Place	Date	Hour	Summary of Events and Information	Remarks and references to Appendices
ANNEQUIN	3/10/15	9.15 p.m.	Early this morning enemy removed "Little Willie" Trench and attacked our front line trenches but were repulsed. During the afternoon registered TRANSVAAL, LONE FARM, AUCHY CEMETERY, LES BRIQUES and HAINES CEMETERY. At 07.30 enemy made an attack in two bursts in front of CITÉ ST ELIE, result unknown. 6.00 pm ordered to prepare to fire on DUMP TRENCH an enemy trench in attack on Big Willie Trench from SOUTH FACE of HOHENZOLLERN	[sig]
ANNEQUIN	4/10/15	9.25 p.m.	Barometer 29.9. Temperature at 8.0 am 43°. Registered "Little Willie" TRENCH, "Boomerang Post" in DUMP-FOSSE 8, CORONS DE PEKIN, CORONS DE MARON. At 2.30 pm ordered to fire 4 rounds per hour at the CORONS. Stay tonight – commenced them at 4.0 pm to they we afford to have lost the whole of HOHENZOLLERN REDOUBT and LITTLE WILLIE	[sig]
ANNEQUIN	5/10/15	5.30 p.m.	Barometer 29.89 Temp 47° at 8.0 am. Wet morning. Continued firing 4 rounds per hour at CORONS	[sig]
ANNEQUIN	6/10/15	8.45 p.m.	Barometer 29.91 Temp 45°. Misty but fine. Ceased firing words per hour at 11.20 pm. 5½ Lachrymose Shells + 16 Incendiary Shell are now stored at the Gun Position	[sig]
ANNEQUIN	7/10/15	9.20 p.m.	Barometer 30.1 Temp 41 at 8.0 am. 7.30 pm Resumed fire at rate of 5 rounds per hour on the CORONS and Communication Trench N.W. of DUMP. No. 4 Gun temporarily out of action	[sig]

WAR DIARY or INTELLIGENCE SUMMARY

Army Form C. 2118

B Battn 1st Brigade RFA

Place	Date	Hour	Summary of Events and Information	Remarks and references to Appendices
ANNEQUIN	8/10/15	9.30 a.m.	Barometer 29.67 Temp 50. at 8.0 a.m. Continued firing 5 rds per hour slowly	
		p.m.	The enemy at the CORONS and in position at TRENCH NW of the DUMP. Enemy began bombarding our trenches to the SOUTH of HOHENZOLLERN towards LOOS about 1.0 p.m. continued till dusk. Reports that they had attacked from North. 5.0 p.m. battery fired 15 rnds gun fire at TRENCH NW of DUMP and also 15 rnds at TRENCH just W of DUMP. Report that enemy were using gas against our TRENCH came in at about 8 p.m. at this hour green + white lights were sent up from HOHENZOLLERN REDOUBT	ShB
ANNEQUIN	9/10/15	9.30 p.m.	Barometer 29.59 Thermometer 50.5, 9 am Continued our normal rate of fire in short bursts. Pro-enemy all this believe... Fired four rounds at point 35 in DUMP TRENCH between 2.0 & 6.0 p.m. At 5.0 p.m. informed that snipers had reached point 42 in DUMP TRENCH. Reports received that enemy's attack yesterday failed completely. Short fury suffered heavily from artillery, machine gun fire. 2" Lieut M A SAUNDERS joined battery. Changed 50 rds per gun - making 98 rds per gun at Sun Parton	(sd)
ANNEQUIN	10/10/15	9.0 p.m.	Barometer 29.58. Temperature 52. Wind NE fine. Registered MADAGASCAR and LITTLE WILLIE trenches also MAD POINT and MADAGASCAR TRENCH. At 7.15 pm fired on (PENTAGON) Communication Trench NW of DUMP - 31 rounds. Continued firing the normal 5 rounds per hour on the CORONS Etc. Dust of the enemy in the CORONS all day in DUMP.	ShB

1875 Wt. W593/826 1,000,000 4/15 J.B.C. & A. A.D.S.S./Forms/C. 2118.

WAR DIARY or INTELLIGENCE SUMMARY

Army Form C. 2118

C.B. Pottinger 130 Brigade R.F.A.

Place	Date	Hour	Summary of Events and Information	Remarks and references to Appendices
ANNEQUIN	11/10/15	9.15 p.m.	Barom. 29.58. Temperature 48. at 8.0 am. Wind S.E. light. at 8.45 a German albatross Biplane was brought down by a British (a British aeroplane). The German came over the battery. Whilst more than 1000 feet high, the machine was hit in the radiator. at 4.0 p.m. two German planes flew over and both got away, on dropping white lights in front of our line side of the CAMBRIN ROAD. Registered the PENTAGON from monn. at R.N.W. and continued the normal rate of fire at PENTAGON. Received more bombardment on COPENS and TRENCHES leading WEST and SOUTH from the PENTAGON. Received more bombardment until 6.7 p.m. — There shells are provided with a green white steel upper parts the steady in green until burst and spread the rich and are refilled by white casting-steady flashed to general yellow storm & having the old descriptive markings, they take poss. MO 44. S/Lt. Wind S.S.W.	
ANNEQUIN	12/10/15	4.20 p.m.	Barom. 29.61. Temperature 56 at 8.0 am. Registered AUCHY ALLEY at 12 40 pm. Also registered A Battery 130 Bde on NORTHERN HALF OF LITTLE WILLIE at 12 40 pm. Fired at O P on DUMP at 3.55 p.m. Fired on PENTAGON from 4.50 p.m. to 6.15 p.m. Battery fire at 30 seconds for 15 minutes, when 60 seconds interval, as Germans threatened attack on the GUARDS. Three German Planes were brought down yesterday. All observation posts advanced to annum. Observer. (6.50 G.12 Div.) End	
ANNEQUIN	13/1/15	10.15 pm	Barom. 29.70. Temp. 57 at 8.0am. Until 12 noon fired normal rates of fire at the PENTAGON. at 12 noon, in conformance with Grenadiers action attached, in support of infantry attack commencing at 2.0 pm; Opened fire in LITTLE WILLIE TRENCH SOUTH HALF, rate of fire Battery fire 30 secs — until 1.0 pm. From 1.0 pm to 1.45 pm fired 2 pdr east of MADAGASCAR. From 1.45 pm to 2.30 pm. Lachrymatory Shell + from 2.30 pm to 4.0 pm Lyddite again. From 4.0 pm to C Battery front at	X

WAR DIARY or INTELLIGENCE SUMMARY

Army Form C. 2118

B Battery, 13th Bgde. R.F.A.

Place	Date	Hour	Summary of Events and Information	Remarks and references to Appendices
	13th Oct (continued)		AUCHY ALLEY TRENCH, NORTH HALF. At 8.30 p.m. fired 4 prs 12 rounds per howr at the PENTAGON & prepared rounds at FOSSE COTTAGES and SLAG ALLEY. Had little information owing to our Maps when using Fuze Percussion 100. Sergt SIMPSON hit by half timber of the shell exploded in the bore at 8.30 p.m. The shelling bursting at the muzzle. There are 100 also quite many "blinds". Reported in progress to H.Q. 13th Bgde immediate after the incident. Two Bgde. 1 prs of gunshrine but 13th Gunners ... with exposed positions are now singly on the night are not augmented. The Infantry notice seem thrown out further the HOHENZOLLERN REDOUBT. The 46th Division pushed out the attack on HOHENZOLLERN and LITTLE WILLIE with the 12th Division on the RIGHT and the 2nd bomb 7th Division on the LEFT. GAS was used from 1.0 pm to 1.50 pm. WIND being light up to 5.5 W.	Fosse Cottages positions marked in extra detail in TRANSVAAL.
ANNEXURE IV	14/10/15	9.15 pm	Barrels 29.9. Temp 52°. 8.0 a.m. Fired at varying rates of 4 prs from Pentagon to 6 pr Tony Mary. Also fired 24 how at PENTAGON. FOSSE COTTAGES and SLAG ALLEY. Shrapnel reported at 8.30 a.m. HOHENZOLLERN and LITTLE WILLIE held by the enemy except in NORTH FACE. About noon Gdh. Div Infantry bridge 50 yards on our left concentrated on the left of 2nd Bde. Heavy battery (Light Butler (60 pdrs) later shelled with 4.2" H.E. +3 men wounded. Infantry during operation from RE Green & Brown were depending with a lieutenant from the bridge went to visible from WATER TOWERS in both CITE ST ELIE and CITE ST LEONARD. The bridge is also trained on line light those batteries.	
	15 July	9.0 am	Barrels 24.75 Temp 57.70°. 9.50 a.m. the light Artillery removed into May 4th. No 4 gun ... ... One gun sent to ZOSK, at CHOCKE, ordered ... firing 12 SA New Army SCOT. Gun reported at 6 SP 2 A.M.	

WAR DIARY or INTELLIGENCE SUMMARY

Army Form C. 2118

80 Battn 180 Brigade R.F.A.

Place	Date	Hour	Summary of Events and Information	Remarks and references to Appendices
ANNEQUIN	16/Oct/15	9 p.m.	Held WEST FACE of HOHENZOLLERN, a part of LITTLE WILLIE and the greater part of BIG WILLIE. Barometer 29.74. Temperature 50 at 8 a.m. Artillery firing 12 rounds per hour. Changed in opinion on to MADAGASCAR and MAD POINT at same rate of fire.	
ANNEQUIN	17/10/15	9 p.m.	Barometer 29.88. Temperature 45 at 8 a.m. At 5.07 p.m. opened fire on ROAD and RAILWAY N.E. of the DUMP, in support of GUARDS attack on BIG WILLIE & DUMP TRENCH. At 10.0 a.m. returned to harass the DUMP itself as the GUARDS had got back BIG WILLIE but were held up at point 60 6, machine gun fire from the DUMP. At 11.40 p.m. returned rate of fire to N2 per hour. At 8.0 p.m. changed to slow length in last nights MAP POINT and MADAGASCAR. Have fired some previously with great No.3 gun shield badly perforated by hose of shell. No.2 Gunner shield dented. Timing now by transport from outside Gun pit.	X1
ANNEQUIN	18/10/15	9.0 p.m.	Barometer 30.03. Temperature 48. Continued firing 12 rounds per hour at MAD POINT and MADAGASCAR. Ceased firing at 3.30 p.m. Have two men previously lately with 100 per — No further relief from CHOQUES & printed & left at wagon line	
ANNEQUIN	19/10/15	8.30 p.m.	Barometer 30.00. Temperature 41°. 4.30 p.m. No 3 Gun with horse and set forward but with 9.10 p.m. 2nd Lieut SAUNDERS. 5.15 p.m. German made a counter attack on HOHENZOLLERN. Fired in PENTAGON and Sett continued at rate of 12 per hour. B/B1 Battery on section relieved left section at 6.15 p.m. Orders received to withdraw from position yesterday & SERVIA mentioned as destination.	
BAS RIEUX	21/10/15	8.30 a.m.	Left relic marched at 11.0 p.m. Yesterday. 21°. to relieve. 2nd Lieut SAUNDERS injured by trap beam from his horse near CHOQUES and taken to HOSPITAL Lieut MUDIE left in command to MARSEILLES via BETHUNE and PARIS. Report to Brigade Major 28th Div. ARTY. Right section relieved by remaining section 13/61 at 5.45 a.m. Station 317 Relieved but in marched for position at 9.0 p.m. arrived in billets at 11.30 p.m. last night. Their firing occupied when travelling roads at LILLERS & LOTHAM "to Valley" Orders for light at 9.22-23. Right Section Guns put to CHOQUES for orders of crossing year W.O. Signed Major F.L.P. J.B.C. & A. A.D.S.S./Forms/C. 2118. ~ Mobilisation SERVIA confirmed G.S. Wagon to be returned	

WAR DIARY or INTELLIGENCE SUMMARY

Army Form C. 2118

B Battery 130th Bde. R.F.A.

Place	Date	Hour	Summary of Events and Information	Remarks and references to Appendices
RAS RIEUX	22/10	7.15 pm	Right Section Guns returned from CHOCQUES by 4.30 pm. Had Guns & Coffers & horses in the Gun Park by Artillery patter. Right half Battery left Billets for LILLERS Station at 6.30 pm. Remainder will leave at 10.15 pm.	XII
MARSEILLES	24/10	2.10 pm	Left half Battery left LILLERS STATION at 3.0 am. Arrived at AMIENS 10.30 am. LONGEAU 10.30 am. VILLENEUVE St GEORGES 7.30 pm. MONTEREAU 11.30 pm. Arr 24th DIJON 10.30 am. CHALON SUR SAONE 12.40 pm. MACON 2.10 pm. LYON 6.45 pm. VILLEFRANCHE 11.0 pm. 00thRN 25th PIERREPLATTA 2.10 am. MARSEILLES 4.30 am. Detrained proceeded to Parc DU BORELY where the Officers & Men and Company mules came in. Right Section had arrived there before. Weather = raining. No news today.	
MARSEILLE	27/10	3.0 pm	2nd LIEUT N.M.CUNNINGHAM posted to the Battery	
H.M TROOP SHIP KNIGHT TEMPLAR	5/11	9.30 am	Bde Brigade RFA marched from Camp at 7.0 am. On November 3rd and Embarked at MOLE D. MARSEILLES DOCKS in S.S. KNIGHT TEMPLAR. The Ship Sailed at 8.0 pm November 4th. B Battery mounted 2 Screw Guns and A Battery 2 Guns from S	
H.M.T.S KNIGHT TEMPLAR	11/11	10.0 am	Arrived at ALEXANDRIA at 6.0 am. Disembarkhed Horses Vehicles by 10.0 pm.	
MAMURA	12/11	9.0 am	Marched from Docks at 6.30 am through ALEXANDRIA to MAMURA Camp 16 miles EAST of ALEXANDRIA Halted at SIDI BISCHR from 10.30 am to 2.30 pm. Arrived at Camp about 6.30 pm	

WAR DIARY or INTELLIGENCE SUMMARY

Army Form C. 2118

(Erase heading not required.)

Remarks and references to Appendices: 60 Battery 130 Brigade RFA

Place	Date	Hour	Summary of Events and Information
MAMURA	22/11		Lieut. MUDIE appointed actg adjutant in place of Lieut. LAWTON who is ill.
ALEXANDRIA	23/11	11.0	Brigade moved camp to MASARETA in ALEXANDRIA leaving at S.P. am and arriving at 10.30 pm
ALEXANDRIA	24/11		Sent 2 guns to relieve 2 g. A Battery at MASARETA POINT in anti aircraft subdivisional attack (A/A's have returned 2 guns on a large part).
ALEXANDRIA	25/11		2nd Lieut WIMSDEN with 2 guns detachment embarked on transport HORORATA from remounted maindships. One 4.7 Q.F. mounted in the stern.
ALEXANDRIA	26/11		HORORATA sailed this morning. A Battery took this remaining 2 guns embarked on Transport MERCIAN. Relieved A Battery in charge of MASARETA POINT. C Battery relieving 2 guns taken over by A Battery at 1.30 pm
ALEXANDRIA	27/11		2nd Lieut ARMEROD posted to B Battery vice Lieut MUDIE acting adjutant.
ALEXANDRIA	28/11		2nd Lieut JAMES C Battery & 2 guns detachment embarked yesterday proceed to day
ALEXANDRIA	1/12/15	10.0 pm	100 men and 3 guns of C Battery (remainder from cabin at MASASETA POINT) with two officers & two sergeants embarked on S.S. ULYSSES for SALONICA. Rail broken raining
ALEXANDRIA	2/12/15	10.0 pm	1/1st Battery 2nd EAST LANC'S Brigade RFA relieved B.AC Bombyard RFA at MASARETA POINT at 10.30 am.

B Battery

APPENDIX X

Time table of 130 Arts for operations of 13th October

Secret

Battery	Series	Time	Target	Projectile	Rate of fire in rounds per battery per minute	Details of amm^n expenditure
A	1	NOON to 1. PM	N. ½ LITTLE WILLY	Lyddite	2	1 hour at 2 rounds per minute per battery
"	2	1.0 PM " 1.45	AUCHY LA BASSÉE	Lyddite	1.2	¾ " 1
"	3	1.45 PM " 2.0 PM	FOSSE COTTAGES front row	LACHRYMATORY	~~100~~ 120 rounds in ¼ hour	100 rounds LACH^Y in ¼ hour
"	4	2. PM " 5.30 PM	AUCHY LA BASSÉE	Lyddite	2	3½ hrs at 2 rounds per min
						4½ hours at 2 r p m 270 min 540 rounds and 45 [illegible] at 1 r p m. Total 585 lyddite [illegible] lachrymat^y
B	1	NOON to 1 PM	S ½ LITTLE WILLY	Lyddite	2	1 hour at 2 rounds per minute per battery
"	2	1 PM " 1.45 PM	MADAGASCAR	Lyddite	~~[illegible] in ¾ hour~~	¾ " " " " "
"	3	1.45 PM " 2.30 PM	MADAGASCAR	LACHRYMATORY	~~100~~ 90 rounds in ¾ hour	
"	4	2.30 PM " 4.0 PM	MADAGASCAR	LYDDITE	2	1½ hours " " " " "
"	5	4.0 PM " 5.30 PM	N ½ { Trench AUCHY ALLEY A 28.c 4.8 to RL^WY A 28 a 9.8	LYDDITE	2	1½ " " " " " "
						4¾ = 285 min = 570 Lyddite 100 LACHRY
C	1	NOON to 1. PM	Trench A 28 d 4½.2 to 8½.6	LYDDITE	2	1 hour at 2 rounds per minute per battery
"	2	1 PM " 1.45	MAD POINT	LYDDITE	2	¾ " " " " "
"	3	1.45 PM " 2.30 PM	MAD POINT	LACHRYMATORY	~~100~~ rounds in ¾ hr.	
"	4	2.30 PM " 4.0 PM	MAD POINT	LYDDITE	2	1½ " " " " "
"	5	4.0 PM " 5.30 PM	S ½ { Trench AUCHY ALLEY A 28.c 4.8 to A 28.a 9.8	LYDDITE	2	1½ " " " " "
						4¾ hrs = 285 min = 570 Lyddite 100 LACHR^Y

W.S.C.
11/10/15

M.O.1 - Appendix A/   SECRET

O.C. B/130 Brigade R.F.A.

The following minor operations will take place tomorrow the 17th inst.

1. At 5 am the 2nd and 3rd Guards Brigades will commence bombing operations with a view to driving the enemy from BIG WILLIE. The 3rd Brigade will also try to bomb up DUMP TRENCH sufficiently far to cut-off SOUTH FACE.

2. The Heavy Artillery will co-operate

3. Fire on the allotted points will commence at 5 am. Rate of fire for Howitzers, section fire 2 minutes.

4. Programme for 130th Brigade R.F.A. hereto attached.

5. Acknowledge

16th Div

C.C. Clarkin Lt. R.F.A.
Adjt 130 Bde R.F.A.

Reference M.O.1 of 26.IV.15.
Batteries of 130th Brigade R.F.A.
will fire as follows:—

Bty	Target	Rate of fire	Remarks
A/130	A.28.D.9.0. and trenches in front two rows of FOSSE COTTAGES	Section fire 2 minutes	Commencing at 5 a.m. and continuing at same rate of fire until ordered to reduce rate or cease fire
B/130	N.E. of DUMP along road and railway line as far south as SLAG ALLEY	Section fire 2 minutes	"
C/130	PENTAGON	Section fire 2 minutes	"

16 X/XV

Gua Clanten
Lieut R.F.A.
Adjutant 130 Bde R.F.A.

APPENDIX XII

Operation Order No 4
by Lieut-Col H.E. Carey
Commanding 130 Bde RFA

1. The 130th Brigade, less Brigade Am. Col., will march tonight to LILLERS Railway Station to entrain as follows:-

Train No. 11. Bde H.Q., A Battery and ½ B Battery, under the Officer Commanding Brigade, in the above order of march will pass starting point, the present Bde H.Q., at 6.45 p.m.

Train No. 12. ½ B Battery and C Battery order of march as above will pass Bde H.Q. at 10.45 p.m. Capt. Devitt will be in command.

2. The O.C. Bde Am Col will make his own arrangements for entraining tomorrow in accordance with instructions already given.

3. On arrival at Station the O.C. of each train will hand to Staff Capt. a statement showing numbers of Officers, N.C.O.s and men, horses and vehicles, and name of O.C.

4 water carts will be entrained full.

MacLachlan
Lieut R.M.
22/RN   Adjutant- Bo Bde A.P.A

www.ingramcontent.com/pod-product-compliance
Lightning Source LLC
Chambersburg PA
CBHW081441160426
43193CB00013B/2344